THE
nomadic
MINDSET™

NEVER SETTLE . . . for TOO LONG

THEnomadicMINDSET

Advance Praise for *The Nomadic Mindset*™

"Mindset—having the right mindset—is one of the most important success factors of great and inspiring leaders. Kevin Cottam's leadership book seamlessly interconnects ancient nomadic wisdom and today's leadership in a revealing, story-filled book that shares the vital qualities of a nomadic mindset. *The Nomadic Mindset*™ is a necessary read for leaders of all levels traversing today's disruptive environments."

Marshall Goldsmith – Thinkers 50 Ranking: #1 executive coach and the only two-time #1 leadership thinker in the world

"Captivating stories and reminders. *The Nomadic Mindset*™ explores personal leadership qualities essential for good living and well-being in our rapidly changing world. Profiling three typologies—the nomad, the builder, and the settler—this new book makes a compelling case for appreciating and cultivating our ancient nomadic wisdom."

Ron Kaufman – New York Times Bestseller, *Uplifting Service*

"Intriguing and timely! This book brings the wisdom of the nomadic people, who have adapted for centuries to the ever-changing nature, to today's disruptive world and shows us the way to migrate to the new future."

Wendy Tan – *Wholeness in a Disruptive World*

"A book for our time. An opportunity to look forwards to where we need to go in the future while looking back at the wisdom we've lost or ignored from the past. When ancient cultures understand change is paramount to survival, without losing the essence of who they are, that is worth reflecting on. A powerful leadership manifesto that should be a must-read for business leaders everywhere."

Andrea T. Edwards – *The Digital Conversationalist*

"Insightful and inspirational, with engaging stories of travel and meeting interesting people, Kevin takes us on an outer and an inner journey. As humans, we are all intentionally or unintentionally moving from point 'A' to point 'B,' and this book raises some important questions on what leadership is really about—highly recommended."

Andrew Bryant – CSP speaker, coach, *Self-Leadership: How to become a more successful, effective & efficient leader from the inside out*

"A modern era 'nomadic' Robinson Crusoe. Daniel Defoe's epic novel, *Robinson Crusoe*, has been enjoyed by tens of millions of adventurous readers. I believe the same will happen with Kevin's book. The key difference is his book is rich with real people's stories and experiences that we can adopt to *upgrade* our own leadership journey for a storybook life."

Rob Salisbury B.Com. – CSP, Leadership Strategist

"A tour de force of wisdom. This book is *alive*. If you are ready to develop a mindset that is free, curious, and willing to change and adapt to collaborate with the people with whom you share the same space, this is the book you cannot be without to navigate today's complex world."

Dr. Philip Merry – A Leading Expert on Synchronicity and Leadership

Photo by Orgil Batsaikhan

Creative Performance Mastery International Pte Ltd
First Edition 2019

The Nomadic Mindset™: Never Settle . . . for Too Long. Copyright 2019 by Kevin Cottam

Creative Performance Mastery International Pte Ltd
20 Maxwell Rd
09-17 Maxwell House,
Singapore, 069113

ISBN: 978-981-11-7822-1
ISBN: 978-981-11-7824-5 (audio book)
ISBN: 978-981-11-7823-8 (e-book)

Technical Credits:

Structural Editor: Christine Gordon Manley (Manley Mann Media)
Copy editor: Bobbi Beatty (Silver Scroll Services)
Proofreader: Bobbi Beatty (Silver Scroll Services)
Book Cover Designer: Rob Allen (n23art)
Internal Matter Designer: Karl Hunt
Photographers: Hicham Zemmer (Morocco); Orgil Batsaikhan (Mongolia); Kevin Cottam (Maasai, Kenya)
Cover picture: Orgil Batsaikhan
Photo selection and editing: Bojan Tercon
Logo Designer: Anna Bervander (The Forest Studio)
Design Thinkers: Mette Johansson; Jerome Joseph; Kenneth Chase
Guides on the Self-Publishing Journey: Brenda Bence; Andrew Bryant; Pam Wigglesworth; Janet Yung; Kenneth Kwan; Ritu Gupta Merish; Launa Long; Janelle Kwok; plus the many more people who voted and shared their opinions on design, content and support.

www.thenomadicmindset.com

Available from the National Library Board, Singapore Cataloguing-in-Publication-Data.

Order this paperback book or e-book online at Amazon or at www.thenomadicmindset.com.

Printed in Singapore, Singapore 2019

THE
nomadic
MINDSET™

NEVER SETTLE . . . for TOO LONG

Photo by Hicham Zemmer

KEVIN COTTAM

CPMI

Creative Performance Mastery International Pte Ltd

Nomadic Dedication

To my mentor, inspirer, and "inner-theme extractor:"
Fredrik Härén.

To the greatest woman in my life who inspired, supported, and encouraged
me to be a global nomad: my deceased mother Lilian Cottam.

To the so many supporters of this journey.

To Charles de Silva, my friend who put up with
me all these months of writing.

To the executives for their time, wisdom, and conversations.

To the nomads in Mongolia, the Maasai in Kenya, and the
nomads and Berbers of Southern Morocco who have unleashed a deep
purpose inside me stronger than I could have ever imagined.

I have come home.

Ashei Oleng

*Thank you,
in the language of the Maasai people*

Table of Contents

○ ○ ○

PART 1

Direction

○

"Effort and courage are not enough without purpose and direction"

– JOHN F. KENNEDY

Photo by Kevin Cottam

Every journey requires an initial direction. This section is that direction, and it will set the expansive tone for what is to come.

Foreword

A Nomadic Epiphany

Wow! Kevin sure has had a life!

He has had many a-ha moments on the way (as attested to in his first book, *Aha, Mother's Pearls*), and perhaps this latest odyssey has been his biggest. He is a modern nomad. After all, he defines the modern nomadic mindset and lifestyle and understands it from different perspectives, based on his journey of discovery in writing this book.

I suspect Kevin increasingly embraced this during his research, rediscovering himself to a certain extent and redefining how he views the world, business, and leadership. When Kevin explained the concept to me in detail, I was captivated. I immediately saw the link to the modern organisation and how different nomadic mindsets interplay in today's workplace. Intimate learnings from Berber communities, African tribes, and nomadic cultures from Morocco to Mongolia have informed this superb book, linking lessons learned to organisational culture, leadership, management, and the operation of today's global companies. A must-read for forward-looking leaders ready to think differently and less traditionally in this age of disruption and transformation.

As I read the book, I found myself transported to many of these far away cultures, rituals, and rules. I became increasingly excited as many of the lessons resonated with the challenges most leaders face today, from small/medium enterprises to large, multinational companies. This was enhanced for me through Kevin's early history and exploration of nomadic cultures, the way they operate, the way they live, and, ultimately, how the different mindsets uncovered fit like glue into the workplace of today as we tackle the undiscovered country of the #futureofwork.

The nomadic learnings that come from thousands of years of experience, evolution, survival, challenge, and change link so well to the current transformative workplace. These human skills in an increasingly digitally enabled world will bring the best out of you, your organisation, and your people.

If this all resonates, then this book is for you. It's a different take on leadership and organisation, one I feel is needed in a sea of listen-to-me titles, advisories, blogs, posts, and five-point tips for success.

Looking at leadership with a brand-new lens can open opportunity, tangible action, and personal development for leaders and aspiring managers/talent.

This book is your starting point, and Kevin is the expert to help you take that forwards personally and within your organisation. I thank him for opening my eyes as a leader and am delighted to be a part of this journey with him.

Now it's your turn! Embrace your inner nomad like I have done and learn to lead in new, compelling, and proven ways. It could be the game changer you are looking for. . . .

Jeremy Blain

Founder and CEO PerformanceWorks International

○ ○ ○

Introduction

Your Future is Now

The Nomadic Mindset™

○

"It is a seed of a calling and time for change . . . change is necessary for new creation . . . realising this is okay, and a little uncertainty is okay . . . change is natural, the only constant . . . think of it as an opportunity"

– DR. SHEILA PATEL, MEDICAL DIRECTOR, MIND-BODY
MEDICAL GROUP AT THE CHOPRA CENTER, CARLSBAD, USA

JANUARY 2018, TIGHMERT, MOROCCO

One chilly January evening at the Maison d'hôtes Nomades in Tighmert, Morocco, my photographer and I sit on the floor at a low table with a young couple from the Netherlands as we share a simple dinner of camel couscous. The room is made warm and welcoming with beautifully coloured woven carpets and pillows and yellow walls adorned with nomadic art. We talk a while, sharing stories about what we experienced in the Sahara with the nomads. The young lady says to me, "After experiencing some life with the nomads, I feel we have lost the plot on so many levels of humanity, and they seem to have it figured out." My eyes light up and a smile covers my face. She was referring to the ancient nomadic wisdom, their qualities and mindset. Though I was fully immersed in researching *The Nomadic Mindset*™ then, this was an affirmation I was on the right track.

Leadership Problem: We Have Lost the Plot

Usually, a book starts with a desire to solve a problem, create a hero's journey, or offer new awareness on a subject or direction. This book is no different.

With the plethora of leadership books out there, the world doesn't need another leadership book that shares the five or seven or ten steps to successful leadership. As Dr. Patel says, "change is necessary for new creation."

Leadership needs a serious Rethink. I believe, as do many of my colleagues in the coaching, consulting, and speaking world, that leaders are searching for something else: a fresh leadership path or framework, a different lens to see, hear, and understand things with. Why? Because something is just not working today as we enter the fast-paced, ever-changing world of Industry 4.0. What may have worked a hundred years ago, or even ten years ago, does not reflect the changing environment in organisations, politics, markets, or cultures today. A quest now exists for new answers to old problems. As Einstein so astutely said,

> We cannot solve our problems with the same thinking we used when we created them.

Hence, we need new mindsets today that are interconnected and aligned to values, purpose, and vision, with a focus on sustainable systems for this rapidly changing and somewhat "congested-thinking" world.

You might have noticed the world, in general, has become overwhelmingly narrow in mindset, thinking patterns, and actions. There is a growing nationalist mindset around the world, and organisations are having difficulties handling the impending disruptions, changes, and technology. Some say we are migrating towards a precipice, especially when you consider climate change, individual behavioural changes, fake news, social and organisational culture shifts, and the rapid decline in biodiversity. Who knows? Perhaps we are.

In many ways, as the young lady from the Netherlands said, "we have lost the plot"! Have we?

A Leadership Answer

How can "we get back on plot"? One answer is to migrate to expansion. This takes a Leadership Rethink.

In this book, I propose a new path forwards. This is not your typical leadership book, rather, more of a back-to-the-future exploration. By revealing the ancient wisdom of nomads who have sustained themselves for centuries through ongoing disruption, these disruptions can be considered as seeds of a calling to some leadership answers for Industry 4.0. This, in itself, stimulates a growing awareness within and presents you with an opportunity to rethink your leadership style, behaviours, and qualities.

The Nomadic Mindset™ is a fresh, expansive-looking leadership framework path for disruptive and rapidly changing times. It is about achieving a balance between inward, narrow-focused thinking and outward, expansive-thinking. Experience the fluidity of nature that dances back and forth between narrow and expansive states of being. This awareness and fluidity can get you back on track as you adapt and migrate towards leading a more holistic and sustainable organisational culture in the contemporary world. This starts with you, the leader.

Those seeds of a calling led me to exploring the nomadic mindset. Over the course of one year, I set off to discover, not just new territories, but different mindsets—primarily the nomadic mindset. Along the way, I discovered some extra golden nuggets, the builder and settler mindsets. They are also very important as all three mindsets exist inside us all.

My experiences with Mongolian nomads, the Maasai in Kenya, and the nomads and Berbers in Southern Morocco, plus conversations with executives from startups to multinational organisations, have shaped the theme and mapping of this book. They have helped define the nomadic qualities you will find live within you, your organisation, and the whole human race. These valuable insights will have enormous significance for your organisational culture, sustainability, and leadership.

You Will Discover . . .

You may think, from the title of this book, I am referring to wandering the world discovering new territories, working nomadically in different global locations, or learning how to work in or discover other countries. Not quite (Well, maybe a bit . . .).

My focus for this book is centered on what Batgerel Bat, Head of Secretariat for Mongolian National Branding Council, in Mongolia told me. She said, "People think nomad means physical movement from place to place to find new and better pastures to graze. No, nomad means the movement of the mind."

The nomad of the mind is a metaphor for moving from one idea to another, one conversation to another, one negotiation to another, one innovation to another. The nomad *is* the movement or migration from place to place in the mind to discover new and better, greener pastures that enrich us, which leads to new growth and prosperity.

You will discover the qualities associated with the nomadic mindset through stories and metaphors. The colourful nomadic rituals and practices, rich cultures, and vast experiences can enrich and awaken your mindset so you see, hear, and understand not only your leadership style and process, but your organisation, your employees, your organisational culture, and the external world.

Migrating to Expansion

On your journey of discovery, you only need to have the capacity and desire to open your eyes, mind, and heart. This will encourage you to migrate to expansion, which is the opposite of narrowness. Awareness expands you. This, I would assume, is how you became a leader.

Expansion is the underlying breadth of the nomadic mindset; migration is the movement towards the nomadic mindset. You can better understand expansion and migration with the poetic mantra of Binderiya, a student at the National University of Mongolia:

"Think Vastly; Act Narrowly"
Think = Mindset   Vastly = Expansion   Act = Migration   Narrowly = Focus

One way of looking at this is the way Karoli Hindriks of Jobbatical in Estonia, who provides jobs and visas for digital nomads, explains,

> I think what the world needs, as we are sitting with our different mindsets, is to really know how to talk to each other, and I think this is the biggest problem in the world right now. So, if we can somehow bridge that gap to see each other's different viewpoints, that would be really powerful.

1. Are you ready to expand yourself and migrate to different viewpoints on leadership and mindset?
2. Are you ready to unleash the nomad in you?

Migrating to Expansion

there is no beginning to this book
there is no ending to this book

you are migrating
to expansion

there is no beginning to your journey
there is no ending to your journey

you are migrating
to expansion

there is no beginning to your leadership
there is no ending to your leadership

you are migrating
to expansion

migrate to expansion
to live in the nomadic mindset, to never settle . . . for too long.
in your mind, always move, always expand to discover
better routes and greener pastures;
this is where great leaders thrive.

are you ready to migrate to expansion?

take a deep breath, look to your horizons
and step into the nomadic mindset . . .

How to Get the Best out of this Book

This leadership path book is divided into five parts: Direction, Departure, Discovery, Destination, and Distillation to aid your Rethink. You are currently in Part 1: Direction. It is not meant to be a how-to or what-to-do book, yet it gives you many 'how' gems. It is organized to give you rethink questions along with rethink pages at the end of each part to jot down some thoughts and actions.

The principle content exists within Parts Two through Four – Departure, Discovery and Destination. A short wrap-up is in Part 5: Distillation. Whether you're embarking on a physical journey or a symbolic one (perhaps an important meeting, negotiation, or a big keynote), most of us go through these five parts.

Part 2: Departure – When you first head out on a journey, you want some general information about your trip. This part is divided into three Departures: Indulge in the Tea Ceremony, Taste some Nomadic History, and Recognize the Nomadic, Builder, and Settler Mindsets. I recommend, if time permits, that you read Part 2 in one sitting; then take time to rethink/reflect and answer some of the questions on the Rethink pages provided at the end of Part 2.

Part 3: Discovery – This section is divided into nine independent learning days and I encourage you to read one day at a time; then rethink, answer the questions and capture any thoughts on the Rethink pages after Day 3, 6 and 9. Each day is rich in story and offers different qualities of a nomadic mindset while integrating executive case studies and quotes from conversations with executives.

Part 4: Destination – The word "destination" can mean goal or outcome or be the term you use for reaching the end of your journey, project, negotiation, or conversation. There are three Destinations: Believe: Culture is a Pillar, Integrate: the Ability to Sustain Sustainability, and Remember: Never Settle . . . for Too Long. They are broad, defining thoughts and actions, necessary to succeed in Industry 4.0. Feel free to capture your thoughts on the Rethink pages at the end of Part 4.

In the end, you alone decide what you have experienced and learned on any journey. My hope for you is that by reading this five-part mindset exploration, you will be inspired to explore, rethink your current leadership and how it can improve through discovering new pastures, and respect humanity as a sustainable necessity. I invite you to migrate to expansion. Happy Nomading.

Mindset of your Capital
– Binderiya

○ ○ ○

PART **2**

Departure

Photo by Hicham Zemmer

Before you leave on any journey, be it a physical one or a business meeting, conference, or negotiation . . . there are insights, information and "stuff" you need to gather to help prepare for the mysteries and discoveries you may encounter migrating forwards.

The Departure will help you prepare.

Indulge in the Tea Ceremony

Gathering, sharing, and clarifying information about your journey is vital to safeguard the road ahead, and that comes from developing rapport and relationships with others, all accomplished over a good old cup of tea or (coffee).

○

"Tea and sugar are more important than food"

– AISSA DERHEM

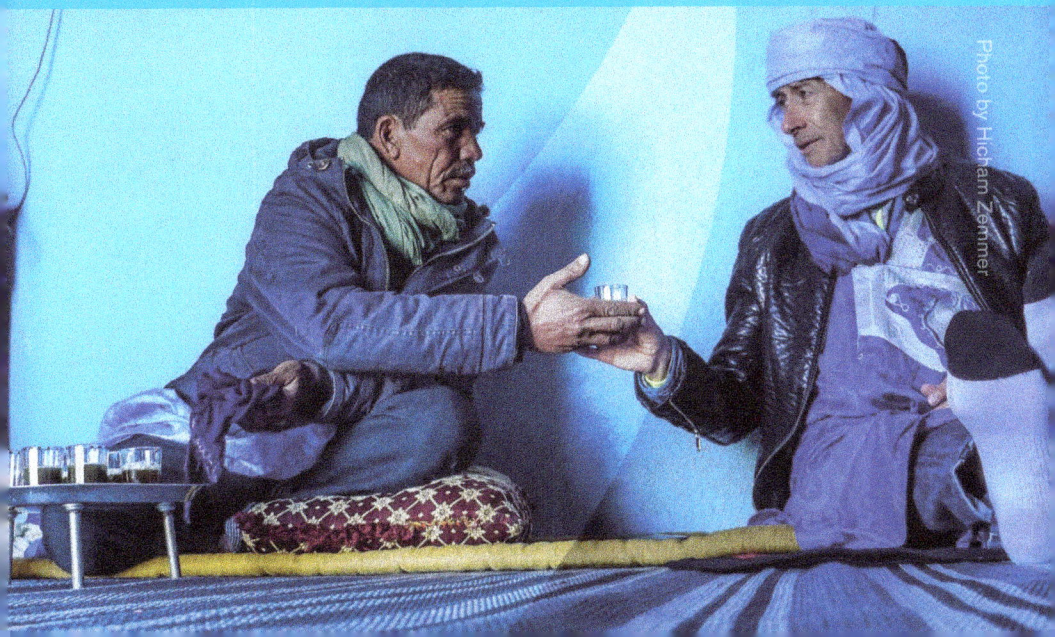

Photo by Hicham Zemmer

JANUARY 5, 2018, TIGHMERT, SOUTHERN MOROCCO

t's chilly, by Moroccan standards (around 5°C), as our group sets off in the early morning from Brahim Tahero's Maison d'hôtes Nomades in an old, rickety 4×4 Jeep. We're driving through the Stony Sahara towards the Atlas Mountains. Our group consists of Hicham (my photographer), Salem (my guide and translator), Mohamed (our driver), and me. We look a little like the Indiana Jones team, dressed in traditional Saharan nomadic clothes of long, flowing blue, white, or black kaftans and turbans, setting off to find the mysterious golden nugget of information that will lead us to the next nugget and then the next till we find the qualities of the nomadic mindset.

Our first stop is the grocery store to purchase welcome gifts: a box of solid, individual, cone-shaped sugar and boxes of green tea. These are the staples of life, Aissa Derhem, a Berber mathematician and social activist (President of the Dar Si Hmad NGO), would tell me later, "Tea and sugar are more important than food."

The Stony Sahara, as the nomads call it, is a grand, open space full of stones, vegetation, and desert that divides the vast, expansive golden sand-duned Sahara Desert we normally see in pictures and movies. Our mission today is to search for nomads and their tents or stone houses.

Our rocky, bumpy experience through this rich landscape reminds me of something I heard on the way to the Maasai Mara in Kenya, "you are having a free African massage." Truly, that is what it is like.

Mohamed hunches over the wheel, driving madly like a Formula 1 driver on a mission, twisting and turning to avoid rocks or to turn onto what may or may not be a road. At the same time, his eyes scan the horizon for nomads and tents. These nomads are true multitaskers with the Eyes of a Hawk, searching the horizon.

❝ I can see much clearer in the desert

Suddenly, the skies open up and we get a downpour, but it isn't long before it dries up and the clouds separate gracefully, allowing the sunshine to appear. This is my first time in the Sahara and a dream come true. The light is brilliantly clear here without pollution, which allows you, literally, to see much clearer with less stress and strain. The nomads say, "I can see much clearer in the desert." I now understand why.

After travelling for two hours, the team approaches the stone, two-room house of Ali Bellini, a herder, and part of his family, in the middle of the Stony Sahara. He has three wives who live in separate locations with their respective five children.

Traditionally, when you arrive at a nomad's tent, whether the visit is expected or not, you are automatically welcomed. Ali greets us as the nomads do, with a handshake and then a lean in to the side of the head, touching heads lightly and switching to the other side. Generally, in traditional Arab cultures, and in this case the nomadic culture, the women are not seen, and only men do the greeting. You do not touch or interact with female nomads in Muslim Morocco, especially in the Sahara, unless there is another male relative with you or them. However, if you go further southwest in Morocco, women are freer and will greet you. Following the initial greeting, the gift giving transaction of green tea and sugar takes place.

Ali leads us into a room where Ali and his family entertain, eat, and sleep. We sit on the floor on colourful, handwoven ethnic carpets and pillows that line the edge of the tent. An open space in the middle allows a few low tables for the food and making of tea.

Now the tea ceremony begins. In many nomadic cultures, and also western cultures, the drinking of tea, coffee, or another drink is an important organisational or cultural tradition. Think of the British, Japanese, and Chinese tea-drinking traditions. This is how the Berbers have conducted business for centuries. My Berber friend, Aissa Derhem, explained that "green tea was a revolution" that *green tea was a revolution* began during the Crimean War of 1856 by the English traders who brought tea to Essaouira, and the caravans of Berbers/nomads transported and traded it across the Sahara and sub-Saharan countries. Before that, he believed the Berbers drank camel milk.

The Tea Ceremony: The Formula for Business and Social Meetings

The way to "good business transactions is through tea," Aissa once told me. The tea ceremony is all about gaining clarity, gathering information, and getting to know each other. It is about building confidence, gaining respect leading to trust, and getting a sense of direction. This is why the Berbers say, "social or business transactions can be dangerous without tea." Tea builds bonds. The choice of Tea Master is very important as he modulates the ceremony (like a leader, host, facilitator, or mediator) to prolong the drinking as long as possible.

Interestingly, I was told that here, often you start with the bad news and end with the good news. In western society, it's more common to use the "sandwich technique" (good news, bad news, good news). The nomadic process starts with the pain/problem of the client, customer, or internal organisational challenge, then follows with a negotiation and positive solution. Rushing the informational gathering process is not a good sign, and the nomads love to take time. Taking time is vital. There's a Berber proverb that says, "you can't put the whole camel in the pot at one time, only one piece at a time" (*Yat s yat urd yat f yat*: one by one not one on the other). Salem once shared this with me, and it means one step at a time, or in this case, one cup of tea at a time.

Modern meetings, especially in the west, are often transactional: too fast and straight to the point, without taking the time to create nuance and build rapport, the relationship, and trust. The getting-to-know-you phase of negotiation is important not only for nomads, but also for constructive business practices and building alliances.

We sit on the floor, without tables, in an open, informal, circular environment so we can observe each other. This is an old tradition and is still done in some parts of the world; however, today, business meetings are more traditionally western-designed with a table and chairs and the leader sitting at the head of the table or in the centre.

Making the Tea

In Morocco, the tea ceremony consists of the following components:

- talking
- brewing the tea
- drinking and eating

I watch in delight as Ali prepares one cup at a time. As Aissa says,

> Not everyone can make tea. You need a good tea master and one who will make the quality last and adapt to the people who are drinking fast or slow. That is why you have to make the first one and then the next and the next.

For the nomads in Morocco, making the tea is an art form, and you want to savour the experience. You need to be practiced and proficient at making sure the foam on the top of the tea is light and frothy and the colour of the tea in the cups is not murky but clear. Many people think of Moroccan tea as the mint tea served globally. That only happens in northern Morocco. In the south, they drink green tea.

While the tea is being made, overflowing plates of fresh dates, almonds, and other nuts are placed on another small table.

The tea tray traditionally has three legs, and each person is given three glasses, not cups, of tea in small glasses that look a bit bigger than a shot glass. (There is significance to the number three, which I'll explain in a bit.)

Ali lines the tea glasses up on the tray. A kettle sits next to him on a burner, and he pours water into a small tea pot. I watch him break off a chunk of sugar from the cone of sugar and stuff it into the little pot. Just watching this makes my sugar level shoot up. Interestingly, in the west, you cater to individual preferences; here, everyone is the same or equal. You wouldn't interfere with the tea master by saying you don't like sugar or please put less sugar in the pot—unless you were diabetic, and then you tell the tea master. That would be a big social faux pas. Don't mess with the tea master.

Then begins the dance of pouring the tea in up and down motions, like a wave, from different heights above the cup. Ali has a great eye for the distance and doesn't spill the tea. The first cup is the darkest, so he pours that into another tea glass, and he keeps "cleaning" and "clearing" by transferring the tea from one cup to the next. This apparently cleans the tea so you can see through it. This process goes on for some time until he feels happy with the clarity of the tea. "Light foam on top and clear tea," Mohamed Billa says, is the perfect tea.

This cleaning, clearing, and getting it just right happens while the tea master chats away. It can take a few minutes to get the first cup of tea right, depending on the proficiency of the tea master. This tea-making process is a good metaphor for a good negotiation or conversation, using what Mohamed Billa told me, "light at the end and clarity fulfilled." It is about cleaning, clearing, and cutting away the extraneous information and slowly getting to the core of the solution. Once the first cup of tea is complete, the whole process starts again.

light at the end and clarity fulfilled 🗨🗨

As I watch this ceremony, I can't help but think of these cups of tea, symbolically. Each cup of tea can be likened to an individual conversation with one person, or a separate idea in a shareholder meeting or speech to your employees. Each cup, thought, or idea must be clean, clear, and have a light froth. That is why you are the tea master . . . a leader.

Drinking the Tea

The first cup is bitter as death, the second is mild as life, and the third is sweet as love.

—Saharan proverb

Ali explains the significance of the three cups. Cup one is strong, cup two is mild, and cup three is light.

As the tea master artfully prepares the tea, I find myself reflecting on how these three cups of tea relate to negotiation. The first cup sets the direction of the negotiation—the big picture or the reason why you are there (the problem or a positive outcome you want to reach). The second cup, after you have developed more rapport and respect, brings you closer to a solution by removing or solving more of the obstacles standing in the way. The third cup can represent the final decision or the few obstacles or hanging issues that might be solved at another sitting.

Regardless of what the meeting is about, developing respect, solidarity, and the relationship is vital to the process. This has been a tradition for hundreds of years with nomads and is still alive today.

The Pivotal Point of Asking Questions

Before our arrival at Ali's tent, Salem told me he would indicate when I could ask my questions. As I sit and observe the body language and listen to the conversations in Arabic, I can see the context is being established between all parties in a relaxed social gathering. It is highly doubtful this conversation would have happened if Salem and the team were not there.

❝ You can ask your questions now

After a while, Salem motions to me and says, "You can ask your questions now."

Now is my moment. Comfortably, I sit with my notebook and pen in hand and turn to Ali and begin to ask him questions about leadership, change, building trust, what is important to a nomad, and more. At one point, he asks me, "What similarities did I find with the different nomadic cultures I had visited for my research?" I smile for a moment and then answer (I ask you, reader, to suspend your curiosity until Part 3: Discovery, when those similarities will be revealed as the qualities of the nomadic mindset.).

Sharing a Meal

Now it was nearing lunchtime. Earlier, Brahim had his cook prepare a picnic lunch for us to take along on our trip. Salem says we will stay and share our lunch with Ali and his three-year-old son. Our offer is gratefully accepted, and one of Ali's wives prepares a delicious camel-maize couscous.

After spending a fruitful few hours with Ali, we say our goodbyes with meaningful smiles. We shake hands, touch heads, and climb back into the 4×4 Jeep. Mohamed, the mad Formula 1 driver, takes off, scanning the horizon for another nomad's tent. The same, but different, process starts all over again with another nomadic family.

The Building Blocks (Qualities) of Relationships

All this sharing, respect, trust, developing rapport, reaching clarity, and gathering information is important, not only in organisations, but in life in general. These are the primary building blocks or qualities of forming strong and impactful relationships and developing partnerships—or not. Sadly, it's easy to lose these building blocks, and it happens so often in cultures today. When we allow ourselves to indulge deeply in gossip, hearsay, the news, political debates, or fake news, we often lose sight of these qualities and our direction—our moral compass. If an entire organisation has lost some, if not all, these qualities, it will most certainly lead to malfunction and poor performance.

Have you ever entered an important meeting where the chairperson—someone you did not know—immediately launched into the business of the day? What did you previously know about them? How did this affect your desire to do business? Now, compare this to a meeting that starts more casually or is led by someone you've already established a trust connection or relationship with. How are the two meetings different? How are you different? *But Kevin*, you say, *I have no time for that nonsense in this fast world of today*. I ask you to seriously think about that statement. What might you be missing, and what could you possibly gain?

There is a better way! I recommend you take a page out of the nomadic book and pour some tea (or your drink of choice). Even when time is in short supply, spend some time (a long time) gathering information, reaching clarity, and developing rapport. I guarantee it'll strengthen your ties, relationships, and partnerships, which will strengthen you, your teams/tribes/clans, client meetings, and organisation overall.

○ ○ ○

LEADERSHIP RETHINK

Essential nomadic leadership qualities to embody:

Rapport	Clarity	Culture
Relationships	Precision	Qualities
Taking time	Respect	Building blocks
Information	Trust	Partnerships
Cleaning	Transference	

FINAL QUESTIONS

1. In most western cultures, it is typical practice to launch directly into business after minor pleasantries. How do you go about reaching clarity? How powerful might it be if you spent time building the relationship first? What might be the advantages and disadvantages for you?

2. Think about the way you gather information or do business. How might you do this differently in the future?

3. How important or useful to you is the concept of the power of three in your leadership and organisation?

Taste some Nomadic History

In preparation for your departure, it is good to know a little history, which will set your imagination afloat in preparation for what is to come. This knowledge will set the scene and open you up to new experiences, a different audience, and potential possibilities and opportunities.

◯

"The way to teach people is through the imagination of learning"

– ROMAIN SIMENEL, FRENCH ANTHROPOLOGIST SPECIALIZING IN BERBER CULTURE

Photo by Orgil Batsaikhan

RETHINK YOUR LAST MEETING

Think back to your last meeting, be it a negotiation, merger, a meeting of your Board of Directors, or a speech to your employees. How did you prepare? What were your intentions? What did you need to know going in? If you were negotiating between two parties, for example, you likely spent some time researching the perspective of the individuals at the table. Perhaps you researched the history of the companies undergoing a merger. Or perhaps your human resources manager spoke to you about employee engagement before your speech to the company.

Understand your Audience

It's part of the journey: understanding your audience. You don't have to know everything, you just have to know enough to sound knowledgeable, enough to engage, and enough to be factual and influential. You do not enter these meetings with zero knowledge—not if you expect to accomplish your goals.

And so it was when undertaking the research for this book.

During my travels to visit the Mongolian Nomads, the Maasai in the Maasai Mara of Kenya, and the Berbers and nomadic tribes in Southern Morocco, I learned much about their lives, including the qualities that represent their lifestyles, behaviours, and mindset. The wise nomads were my audience, and I was their audience in many ways, not only by talking but by observing silently. Now you are my audience. There is still much to discover, which will take the rest of my life, but this is a good start.

What Are Some Definitions of the Word "Nomad"?

Romain Simenel, French Anthropologist specializing in Berber Culture, describes a nomad this way:

> *The best definition for nomads is to state that it's the kind of human mind that is less attached.*

Let's contrast that to the Oxford Dictionary (2018):

> *A member of a people that travels from place to place to find fresh pasture for its animals and has no permanent home.*

Interesting. One focuses on a state of mind, while one focuses on physical movement.

Hema Sedehey, Head of Security Services Business for the Mauritius Commercial Bank, says a nomad is

Somebody who sees life as very transient, always willing to move and very open minded about where you will be in the world.

While Wikipedia (2018) defines a nomad as

A person with no settled home, moving from place to place as a way of obtaining food, finding pasture for livestock, or otherwise making a living. The word Nomad comes from a Greek word that means one who wanders for pasture.

Are you beginning to see a theme here?

Cristian Jonsson, Managing Director at Standard Charter Bank, provides this short but powerful description:

nomad = change

And Robin Lokerman, Group President, MCI-Group, says a nomad is

Somebody who continuously moves and innovates to do things differently.

Yes, there is a theme, with two individual differences, yet they are both about movement. Movement of geographical location and movement of the mind.

"We Were All Nomadic"

Since the beginning of time, people have been nomads roaming the savannah, steppes, deserts, forests, and mountains. As Romain Simenel, states, "We were all nomadic." There are still remnants of this that exist within our DNA even though factors such as industrialization, governments, economies, and education have removed this nomadic mindset from us urbanites. As you read this book, the challenge for you to consider is what is that nomadism within you? Maybe you will begin to feel and become aware of a nomadic rumble inside you.

Most of the world's populace doesn't move. And when you think "move," you probably think of a geographical movement. However, when I was in Mongolia, Batgerel Bat of the National Branding Council of Mongolia said,

"Most people think nomad means moving from place to place. No, it means the movement of the mind." Eureka! That's the meaning this book uses: nomad = the movement of the mind.

In contemporary society, the nomadic mindset is making a comeback in the form of digital nomads, and it has existed for years in the "expat" lifestyle and for those who've "gotten off the grid." These movements, while considered *modern* by some, are actually an evolution of something that's always been within us. The nomadic evolution.

> *Most people think nomad means moving from place to place. No, it means the movement of the mind* 🗣

Anthropology: Nomadic Groups

Nomads can be divided into three main different groups:

- hunters and gatherers
- pastoralists
- peripatetic nomads

You've likely heard of the first two groups. Hunters and gatherers are those who hunt animals and gather berries, herbs, and other natural foods; whereas, pastoralists have herds of animals such as cows, sheep, goats, camels, and perhaps chickens used for food, milk, and currency. The pastoralists sell products associated with their animals: skin, hair, milk, and the whole animal. Peripatetic nomads are generally urbanized and sell crafts and services to the residential population, such as the Roma gypsies do.

For the purposes of this book, the research is centred solely on pastoralists.

Pastoralism and Survival

The early beginnings of pastoralism have been documented to between 8500 and 6500 B.C.E. in the area of Palestine, Israel, Jordan, and southern Lebanon and Syria. These nomads lived in groups of closely knit families in specific areas that moved together looking for grazing land for their livestock, hence their survival (Wikipedia 2018).

Survival is their baseline of life, and this holds true all of us, doesn't it? Yet some humans in contemporary society have forgotten that what we are working for—survival: a roof over our heads, food in our mouths, clothes on our backs—sometimes requires us to move to another location or a new company so we can provide the basics of life. Organisations are no different; survival is about staying profitable, being successful, and surviving the onslaught of competition.

For many, we've forgotten, or lost track of, this notion of survival due to consumerism, being comfortable, and greed, which can potentially lead to corruption. Lest we forget, in theory, life on the baseline is about survival, and that is what true nomads are faced with on a daily basis.

There are, of course, people who do focus solely on their survival. In contemporary society, we may not have to fear wild animals chasing us (usually) or rival tribes launching attacks; however, there are people living on or below the poverty line, and they often depend on handouts. They know about survival firsthand. We also see this in gangs, drug addiction, and wars. In organisations, you see this when the market declines or a global trade war or competition is severe. It is all survival in different forms.

To help avoid devastation, nomads will often intermarry to extend and develop broader kinship and community. This directly increases the support from a larger community of related families; hence, the network of survival and business opportunities grows. Likewise, companies develop partnerships, mergers, or old family businesses to increase safety, loyalty, networks, and greater opportunities.

No matter what part of the world you are in, nomads are connected with nature and their surroundings and flow as one with the animals, land, climate, universe, and other human beings. As a Maasai woman, Lilian, told me, one of the Maasai's greatest qualities is unity. Unity is vital for their survival as a tribe and their culture. Where is the unity today in your organisation or in the world in general?

Modern Pastoralism, Mongolian Style

Tuya Shagdar, a social anthropologist from the National University of Mongolia, helped me understand the Mongolian nomadic history during the Russian occupation (1924–1992), which is very different than that of the Berbers or the Maasai.

She says that "nomads are not endlessly wandering people and settle in areas for periods of time during the year. It is a myth, or perhaps a romantic notion, that nomads wander endlessly, especially today. Nomads are strategic in their movements."

Tuya continues, "the land in Mongolia is vast, allocated, and planned due to the special ecosystem and the need to graze on large swaths of land. Therefore, allocation and wandering, or moving, is specifically planned during winter and spring."

During Soviet Occupation

Under the Russian Soviet system, there were two stages of pastoralism. In the first stage, before 1960, the socialist system of animal and land collectivization didn't fully consider Mongolia's fragile ecosystem. All the animals were state owned, not privately owned by nomads as they were before occupation. The ecosystem and the nomad people's economic base are finely intertwined and strategic.

The Russians didn't take this into consideration and realised the socialist practices that worked elsewhere didn't fit in Mongolia. Though the nomads were allowed to herd and migrate their animals in the different seasons, the state owned the animals, and the nomads were given a small stipend for herding them. Many nomads during this period moved to the cities to earn money as being a nomad was not financially viable or highly regarded. It changed their lifestyles greatly.

The Russians then entered stage two when they realised they needed to be more flexible to motivate herders. They allowed households to have their own small stock of animals, thereby enabling the nomads to financially gain from personal ownership, which resulted in more engagement and independence. This was beneficial especially during a *dzud*, or harsh winter. Financial assistance in this system was heavily subsidized by the government, which provided hay and shelter, especially during winter periods when the ground was too hard.

Post-Soviet Occupation

After the collapse of the Soviet Union, the system too collapsed, and with it the subsidization, and the nomads were now on their own. As the country struggled economically, many of the nomads and professionals that had become urbanized returned to the countryside and became herders again. Today, more and more herders are returning to Ulan Bator and living in their yurts.

we count livestock more than the people 🢅🢅

Nergui Sandagjav, CEO of Reach Finance MFI, in Mongolia, which supports and offers microfinancing to Mongolian nomads, says "we count livestock more than the people." During the Soviet era, the government's focus was to reach a goal of thirty million animals in the country, which they never did.

Since privatization, the number has grown to sixty million animals. She jokes that "the government does an animal census each year and only every ten years for people."

When you think of your organisation and look at where the Russian system went wrong, one of the major factors was independent ownership and the responsibility that engages and motivates the nomads. In what ways does this relate to how you drive or build engagement, resilience, and motivation with your employees and leadership? Perhaps it is in giving your employees more freedom and less boundaries, letting them be more independent while remaining interconnected units, or encouraging them by recognizing them?

Comparing Kenya, Morocco, and Mongolia

Today, a form of collectivization exists whereby the nomads pay a rental fee for different locations during the year. This is the reality for the Maasai in Kenya, who have given up much of their land to collectives overseen by large companies. Yet, if the Maasai have money, they can purchase (and are purchasing) land (my Maasai brother, Joel Soit, was proud to take me to his purchased land to visit one of his wives and children there). These changes continue to be a disruption for the nomads in a variety of countries.

In Morocco, the nomads can roam the Sahara within Morocco itself. Due to current geographical borders and terrorism, it has become challenging for them to roam large swaths of land east and south of Morocco.

Nomadism today is alive and well in Mongolia, and the people enjoy this lifestyle even with the technology of today: solar panels, computers, TVs, fridges, and mobile phones. It seems somewhat incongruous; however, the technology, they say, makes their life easier in many ways. With mobile phones, they can stay in direct contact with their children and families in the cities; solar panels give them electricity for light and a freezer to freeze milk and meat for the winter months; cars and motorbikes result in more agility, so they can achieve things faster and herd their animals in a not-so-traditional way.

The Maasai have not advanced as much as the Mongolians regarding technology, yet they are slowly changing and adapting. When I asked my Maasai brother how he charged his roughed-up clamshell phone, he happily showed me a tiny solar panel about the size of a large Samsung phone sitting on the top of his dung hut, with a wire that led into the hut, directly to his mobile phone sitting on the bed.

Of the three nomadic cultures, the Maasai appear to have the worse financial and living standard than others. Sadly, it appears the government seems to sideline them.

Detached and Free

As Romain Simenel says, "nomads are less attached to material things than we are in the majority of the world," which allows them to move quicker, make decisions faster, come up with more ideas, and be nimbler. They are freer in their mindset and that is their spirit—to be free. Romain explains, "compared to other humans, nomads are completely free in space. You decide. Nobody decides for you what is your destination."

Romain's thoughts on material attachment may seem curious to us. He says, "this specifically means that they have no land." That's important because the notion of owning property is foreign to nomadic cultures in Mongolia, Kenya, and Morocco. They believe the land belongs to everyone as it is given by God. It is a sharing. Therefore, no one can own it. This is a foreign concept for most of the world today. While some ownership is occurring now, this is an adaption to a new disruption.

nomads are less attached to material things than we are in the majority of the world **"**

What pastoral nomads are attached to, though, is their animals—their camels, horses, cows, goats, and sheep—as they are their transportation, business, and livelihood.

In many ways, this no different from an organisation because they have products and services. The nomads have a deep spiritual connection and gratitude to their animals. Can you say the same about your company and its products and services? What is your deep connection to your products and services—and the humans that work for and with you?

Changing Existence

True pastoralist nomads are declining in most parts of the world. This is often due to governments wanting to control their movement so they can tax them, take their land away from them for tourism, or convert their land into crops, hence forcing nomadic cultures into permanent settlements. There are many reasons.

Sadly, though, history has shown the "civilized societies" have failed in their responsibilities to humankind and not fully recognized the value of the nomadic peoples, their richness of culture, family kinship, and qualities that can assist our lives, leadership, and business today. Examples of this can be seen in governments harnessing the people and putting the indigenous peoples of North America and Australia into reservations and residential schools. This has eroded their spirits, cultures, languages, and societal relationships, which has destroyed and separated families. This in many ways has literally taken their lives from them. One can only hope for true change, acceptance, and forgiveness to be bestowed upon the indigenous peoples and nomads around the world.

Nomads = Business = Tribes

Nomads are always in tribes. Wherever there are nomads on this planet, there are tribes.

– Romain Simenel

Romain told me that business was first started by nomads (globally) who traded with others in the Sahara, and then the Berbers began with trading the business products of gold and salt, which the nomads would bring by camel to markets to trade and sell for currency. They also traded antimony (also known as kohl). Kohl appears black but is actually a deep blue, a symbolic colour of the nomadic traditions as it represents the sky. It is not only used as a beauty product when put around the eyes, but it also cures against the impurities of the sand, dust, and everything else that exists in the desert.

As French, English, and Portuguese explorers appeared in Morocco between the fourteenth and sixteenth centuries, the nomads traded with the explorers, thus conducting business. This was the first time Europeans and Saharan nomads connected with each other.

Consider the word "tribe." Chances are you use that word yourself even though you do not belong to a nomadic tribe. Think about your organisation and what you call your teams. In the digital world, the term "tribe" is often used to refer to those who are alike.

Therefore, a tribe is known to be a group of self-sufficient people who live together, sharing a common land who are different from the mainstream culture of a nation (such as indigenous people). On the other hand, a "clan" is a group of people united by kinship relationships. Sometimes the whole organisation is the tribe, and within it, the teams are the clans that interconnect. In the nomadic world, clans are somewhat autonomous yet interconnected to other clans when dealing with big issues or decisions that need to be made. This is where kinship sharing is vital for communication and functioning as a whole.

In some corporate tribes, a culture of hoarding and protecting information is promoted. This can lead to isolation, poor communication, excessive control, secrecy, unnecessary competition, protecting ideas, and insecurity. The best organisations share information and interconnect their creativity, innovation, and ideas, leading them to promote many positive attributes (such as trust, respect, motivation, engagement, and confidence). Referring back to the nomads and their communities, sharing is vital for survival, as it is for organisations, as it develops kinship and a more powerful team. It is more about the "we" rather than the "I." Consider your company and how you promote information sharing.

Now think about your company and how much time, energy, motivation, and financial waste can be improved if you share information within your tribes, clans, or teams? Sharing information between tribes or clans stimulates understanding, harmony, and a road to faster progress (think tea ceremony!), which is the opposite of what happens in many organisations.

You as the Leader

The seeds of leadership existed holistically within the nomadic people. I believe, from my research with nomads and executives, that if you can use some of the qualities of a nomadic mindset in leadership, your organisation will become more aware, engaged, successful, and humanity driven, giving you access to the real talents and qualities of your employees. This motivation and vision comes from the top.

Here are some suggestions of possible comparisons for you to consider:

- New pastures represent the new in your company, whether these are new opportunities, products, innovations, customers, partners, or something else "new."
- Leave a pasture before it is too late. Have the insight to see and know when a product, a territory, an idea, or an employee is nearing the end, not working out, or becoming a financial drain. Let go and move on.
- Survival is an organisational baseline. Look at what this means, regularly, from a sales, marketing, humanity, and visionary perspective, ensuring all is aligned and you have the ability to adapt and shift direction when needed.
- Kinship is vital for your company to flourish. This means focusing on enhancing shared relationships within and without at all levels.
- Build small, autonomous, interconnected communities internally as well as externally. Promote teams, tribes, or clans to cross-pollinate through networking and sharing new ideas, which will motivate and inspire voices to be heard.
- There is no room for being static. Every working part of your organisation should be in a state of constant movement and change. Embrace the interconnectivity of things.

- Encourage the migration of your employees from one position to another, from one idea to another, from one thinking pattern to another, from one location to another.
- Inspire personal and team ownership by encouraging employees to take direct responsibility for their actions and thoughts by stimulating the nomadic mindset.

As you travel on your journey to the nomadic mindset, consider history by connecting the dots of the evolution of your organisation, relationships, partnerships, and leadership styles.

While doing that, you might notice different mindset typologies of individuals or the different mindsets that were driving your institution at different points of your evolution. The next chapter will introduce to you three different mindset typologies vital for you as a leader to take a strong and committed look at. This will help you discover your personal dominant mindset typology and that of those in your corporation.

○ ○ ○

LEADERSHIP RETHINK

Essential nomadic leadership qualities to embody:

Tribes	Knowledge	Movement of the mind
Clans	Skills	Autonomy
Teams	Understanding others	Kinship
Sharing		
Educating	Change	Listening
Connect the dots	Disruption	Patience
Relationships	Independence	Gathering

FINAL QUESTIONS

1. Consider the history of your organisation, connecting the dots of what worked and what didn't work. As you move to future possibilities, what would you do differently?

2. Does your organisation operate in tribes/clans? How so? Do they communicate and share information together? Do you reach outside your organisation to other tribes? What might this do for you if you did?

3. How can you stimulate/motivate your tribes to think more nomadically in your organisations?

Recognise the Nomadic, Builder, and Settler Mindsets

On your journey in your workplace, negotiations, life—indeed everywhere—you will encounter different people with different mindsets. It is important to understand your dominant mindset first and then others'—if you can—so communication, understanding, awareness, and flexibility can be realised to its fullest potential.

○

"Nomad means the movement of the mind."
**– BATGEREL BAT, HEAD OF SECRETARIAT,
MONGOLIAN NATIONAL BRANDING COUNCIL**

Photo by Kevin Cottam

DISCOVERING THE DIFFERENT MINDSETS

Through interviewing anthropologists, executives, and individuals in the learning and development fields, as well as observing and experiencing life with nomads, I discovered some exciting golden nuggets beneficial for you to reflect upon. They are the three different mindset typologies: the settler, builder, and nomadic mindsets. My interviews were fundamental in collectively creating a list of qualities, behaviours, and sample avatars that can be associated with these typologies.

But before we get into all that . . . why is it important to understand these mindsets in the first place?

The Mindset in Organisational Evolution

Leadership is being shaken up today, not only organizationally, but politically as well. Why? Because, as Robin Alfred, CEO and Founding Director, Findhorn Consultancy Service, who has done extensive work for many organisations on sustainability and conscious, intentional leadership, says, the old ways and paradigms of the past are not necessarily working today. As Robin asserts,

> Leadership needs the freshness of the mindset of the future. It (the nomadic mindset) gives you a map and a future possibility on how to examine, and not only recognize your dominant mindset, but see your whole organisation and current and potential clients with fresh eyes.
>
> Most leaders are focused on what they have been taught in business schools and leadership courses on vision and mission and five-year strategic plans. However, in Frederik Laloux's book, *Reinventing Organisations* (the most influential management book in the past decade), Laloux explains this is not the right paradigm anymore. It is more sense and respond rather than plan and control.
>
> Not so many leaders are working at that level in my experience. I think what people are being taught in business schools is not this type of thing. It is still old school where here's how you do spreadsheets, financial planning, marketing. It is not fresh. It is not meeting where we are, and it is not creating the future with a future-based mindset. It is creating a future based on a historic past set of paradigms.

Therefore, developing an awareness of these different typologies (settler, builder, and nomadic) will enable you to better identify the mindsets you already have or the awareness upgrade needed in your organisation at different times of its evolution by always having an eye on the future.

Understanding Assessments

As in many different personality or behavioural assessments, a generalized sampling of a broad variety of qualities, behaviours, and characteristics of different people, cultures, and societies are captured. The typologies of these mindsets are no different. There is often overlap in their defining typologies, as there is with those in this book. I caution you to look at them from an expansive perspective, understanding that not one size fits all individuals or institutions. Robin speaks about this and its potential usage.

It is not about jettisoning one mindset or another, it is about transitioning or including one of the different mindsets into the way of aware thinking. For example, if I am a leader and want to grow my people, the more I know [about] where they sit naturally, [the more] I can help to expand their awareness and lead them to create and embrace broader perspectives. So if you are a settler and if I put you in a settler position, if you want to develop the side of you which is a builder or a nomad, then this can give a sense of personal and career development process or a map for personal development.

The Value of Mapping

Mapping is helpful when observing, communicating, and working with others. It develops a greater understanding of self and others. Robin expresses this well.

I think it can be useful to map my own organisation and other organisations and see potential collaborators, competitors. I can see where potential conflicts might emerge, not necessarily because of conflict, but more around mindset. If I am aware of the mindsets of people when we are in dialogue, then I can look at the field I am part of and say if this is where my organisation is in respect to these mindsets. For example, Apple, Samsung, and Nokia—what are the mindsets operating there? What collaboration can become possible or what do I have to watch out for? It can give a mapping of what is around me: threats and successes.

You have all three mindsets swimming around inside you, as does everyone in your company and everyone around you. It is important, then, to recognize that in your organization, you need a balance of all three mindsets to be successful. They are all needed and important.

What are the threats and risks if a corporation consists of only one dominant mindset typology? The short answer is this: A dinosaur just might appear!

Innovate or Dinosaur?

It is also wise to recognize that during an organisation's evolution, it will go through different stages or phases associated with these mindsets. This is dependent on a variety of factors, such as the vision of the company and CEO, long-term objectives versus short-term, market share, innovation, needs of the outside world, politics, and more.

Sometimes you will have a nomadic phase and will then settle and build or vice versa. The red flags start to go up when you settle for too long. Then it might be too late for your company and extinction may begin. This has happened in many companies, even great ones such as Kodak, Nokia, Toys 'R Us, Sears, MySpace, and Borders.

Kodak, for example, was the great creator of film and the "Kodak Moment." Hugely successful, after 128 years, the world's largest film company claimed bankruptcy in 2012 (Usborne 2012). It became a dinosaur as people were not using film anymore, choosing, instead, digital cameras. If we track its historical dominant mindset typologies, we can see they were once great nomads and then built (builder mindset) on this success for years, maintaining the bulk of global market share for decades. In 1975, a scientist/innovator at Kodak designed and presented the first digital camera (nomadic mindset). It was not accepted by leadership as it would dampen their film business, so they didn't create it (settler mindset). They didn't believe in the new pastures as they were holding onto the past (settler mindset). Ultimately, they were too late. The digital space was too far ahead, they lost massive market share, and, they became a dinosaur.

Companies like Kodak all started with a nomadic mindset, experiencing success with their mandate, vision, and products. They built and built on this initial vision with adaptations during their evolution. Then settlement set in due to a variety of factors such as complacency, potential ego, loss of vision, shareholder value, leadership holding onto the past and becoming comfortable in the market space they owned, and pressure for quarterly returns and growth numbers.

Generally, these corporations have fallen into the numbers traps and forgotten to peer into their crystal ball to find new pastures ahead, i.e., using only narrow thinking. Then new players were born and the old players that had settled were generally not flexible, adaptive, or fast enough to transition back to a nomadic mindset again. Hence, the key players became dinosaurs.

Do you want this for your organisation? I don't think so.

The Mindset of the Leader

From my research, and as all those in the leadership space suggest, the biggest deciding factor in the success of an organisation in today's rapidly changing disruptive environment is the intrinsic dominant mindset of the leader, leadership team, and board of directors. This must then cascade from the top downwards, keeping in mind the extrinsic mindset risks and threats.

The questions are, are you nimble enough to change direction, and how fast can you move? How fast can you pack your bags and move to the next destination like a nomad without letting go of the successful parts of your corporation? Is your thinking expansive enough or too narrow? Or, is it not fluid enough to flow from expansion to narrowness and back again?

> **❝ Nomads 'think vastly; act narrowly,'**

In Ulan Bator, I met a wonderfully astute, young millennial student, Binderiya, who said, "Nomads 'think vastly; act narrowly,'" which I mentioned earlier. When considering a strategic move, a new location, or the welfare of their livestock, a nomad thinks and sees with an open and wide view of the situation (thinking vastly), and then makes a plan, a decision, and zeros in with intense focus (acting narrowly), realising the risks that might be at stake. This happens quickly.

With this in mind, let's have a look at these mindsets with an open mind as a way of mapping your organisation and yourself to find what is needed for now, Industry 4.0, and for the future. Your journey begins now.

Mapping the Individual Typologies

When considering these typologies, remember there is a spectrum of extremes within each typology and the qualities or behaviours within each person who exhibits a specific dominant mindset. One person may be more fearful than another, less caring, more demanding/arrogant, more innovative, or less able to embrace change easily, etc. Personalities vary, so the variables are immense.

The qualities can be referred to as values, beliefs, and behaviours. Like all the mindsets, they are formed through family, education, politics, peer groups, societal norms, age, needs, etc. There is no right or wrong way to see a mindset.

Your dominant mindset might be beneficial in some situations and a hindrance in others. For example, you may be settled in the way you approach finances and hate the risk of the stock market, yet you may be innovative when it comes to new products, ideas, and leadership. Simply put, everyone has an overall dominant mindset, and this can change over time.

Readers Caveat!

I want to be careful not to give you the impression that there is a hierarchal order, a particular bias, or one mindset more important than another. That will be your decision in the way you look at them, and it depends on many factors such as culture, class, education, physical geography (urban versus rural), and more (Although, you will discover a particular bias towards the nomadic mindset qualities in Part 3: Discovery.)

As you read through the list of qualities and behaviours, one to thing to remember is that some strengths or shadows are situational and may or may not apply to you. There is variance: "think vastly and act narrowly."

Typology 1: The Settler Mindset

> *You need glue people in any organisation, otherwise you have chaos.*
> *– John Russell, Managing Director of North Head, Beijing China*

The settler mindset is the glue John Russell is speaking about in the quote above. This is the most prevalent mindset on the planet. Russell's global corporate knowledge helped me understand the important place the settler mindset has in societies and organisations to keep the systems humming through all the ups, downs, bumps, and grinds. I am confident the connotation and meaning of the word "settler," has caused images and thoughts to rise within you.

> *A settler is someone who makes a nest, creates a space that is welcoming, supportive, caring, more people orientated . . . a relational space, the base from where I journey [that] creates structure that is [about] belonging, nurturing, focusing more on the belonging than the becoming.*
> *– Robin Alfred, CEO and Founding Director,*
> *Findhorn Consultancy Service*

Historically, nomads migrated around the world or from pasture to pasture before settlers came into existence. The settlers came about as people would migrate to one location and begin to build a life for themselves and their families. They would settle and harvest the land, trade in communities, and hold the fort, so to speak, while "nomads" within the community would go out and seek new land or trade or even make war. This is what you see in today's world, and in nomadic cultures, where they have settled and become comfortable with their surroundings, products, daily activities, and social networks.

The settler to me is someone that gets comfort out of staying nested, so they build kind of an environment around them, and they are most comfortable in that level of competence, which might not end up being competent because you are not evolving. I think the settler is closer to that status quo, which is the value of keeping things as they are and maintaining the protected lands, protecting the community, and [being] comfortable with the way things are.

– Claire Smith, VP Sales and Marketing,
Vancouver Convention Centre

If you recognise your organization, or others, are in this mindset, you may want to question your vision or direction for the future because an organisation with a settler mindset is not going anywhere rapidly—they are greatly influenced by their dominant qualities to resist change and avoid potential risks. A person with a settler mindset is comfortable with the status quo. And this is all okay! As a leader, you just need to know this and help your settler employees slowly shift their thinking patterns to expand their horizons—if you can.

A person with a settler mindset is here for the long term with deeply rooted connections within the organisation. They will always be grounding themselves and can be ambitious, but within the context of their own country, community, or organisation. They tend to bend their behaviour to be accepted, so they can grow in that space.

– Hema Sedahey, Head of Security Services,
Mauritius Commercial Bank

Potential Avatar of a Settler Mindset

Employee "A" (the settler) shares their story with a human resources director:
I was born in this community and have only lived here. I don't have a lot of interest in venturing too far because my community is rich, and I feel comfortable in my surroundings. Things don't change much around here, which I like

a lot because it is predictable, and that makes me feel safe. I like to do things in my own little way as this makes me more efficient. My whole family lives here and has for many generations. Our little house we have had since the beginning of our now 20-year marriage.

My focus is community and family, and what I enjoy about working in a company is team spirit. I am very diligent and committed to 9 to 5. When I work, I am systematic and do it repetitively as that gives me great comfort. It is rare that I am sick, so you can rely on me. I am grateful such a big company has set up here because I am not moving and [am] yours for the long term. What my attributes are for staying the long course for you is that my organisational history is vast, and I am able then to engage with new employees with joy to help nurture their talents. I am not that keen on taking on movements up the ladder as I am comfortable in my position. I am certainly keen to learn, yet what makes me nervous is change, doing things that I don't know, and asking me to lead or make decisions.

> *When I work, I am systematic and do it repetitively as that gives me great comfort.* 🎧

Qualities and Characteristics of the Settler Mindset

As you read through this description, you might identify people and institutions in this dominant mindset. Be careful, though, not to judge people with different mindsets and label them as is the tendency with typology assessments. Remember this is a mapping tool that allows for more awareness, leading you to make strategic decisions on a variety of issues. Below are few of the qualities associated with the settler mindset.

STRENGTHS

- are the glue and stability of the organisation
- like a repetitive task
- are content
- are predictable
- enjoy doing a job well
- are loyal
- are 9-to-5 workers, rarely more
- have an institutional memory and history
- are empathetic
- are detailed

SHADOW SIDE

- are resistant to change
- are risk averse
- are often narrow thinkers
- are fearful
- work in silos
- are attached to established ways

- are slow moving, can slow down processes
- can complain and spoil things
- want a fixed place to work in
- rarely journey or travel outside the nest

If you identify as a settler, you may disagree or not relate to or identify with some of the strengths or shadow qualities. That is all well and good because these are general qualities and behaviours that *can* show up, not necessarily *will*. In fact, you may also identify with qualities of the builder and nomadic mindset typologies. If you have an uncomfortable response to some of the qualities, though, I encourage you to muse and ask yourself tough questions, such as is your response true or false and what do you need to do to change your view of that quality?

1. When you look at your organisation, can you mentally identify who the settlers might be? If so, how?
2. In what ways do your settlers add value to your corporation?
3. What are some ways you can communicate better with those with a dominant settler mindset typology?

Typology 2: The Builder Mindset

The builder mindset should be the one that drives the operations because they're the ones that say 'we know what we're gonna do: let's do it really, really well.'
– Steen Puggaard, Investor and Former CEO 4 Fingers Crispy Chicken

If the settler mindset is the most prominent mindset on the planet, the builder mindset is a close second. As the word "builder" suggests, this mindset is one that builds—they consider themselves or their company in a state of evolving.

The builders are certainly the ones that you need in medium stages. These are people that are well-needed because they are responsible. They are the ones that really know how to manage processes, build relationships with the different stakeholders, and have the capacity to move our objectives forwards in a way that allows our organisation to be steady, going into the right direction.

– Genoveva Ruiz Calavera, Director of the
Western Balkans, European Commission

The builder mindset is truly representative of the C-suite—but can also appear in other roles—of an organization, such as the COO, CTO, CIO, and CFO (sometimes), who are taking the vision and cascading it downwards, or laterally, to managers, who put it into action through teams, departments, sales, production, and marketing. They strategically make choices that will develop and grow the corporation. What happens, though, in many institutions, is that the cascade gets stuck at the top or at the management levels.

With a builder mindset, you take long-term perspectives and build out in one location or one focus of endeavour. It is the builders that build the cities and the nomads don't—builders take great pride and self-worth in digging deep to whatever [they] are doing—they are the pillars of society. [In] company sector culture, they almost tend to have attributes for focus— styles of friendships and community.

– John Russell, MD North Head

Those with a dominant builder mindset can be incrementalists, which means they look at each detail and work on the bits and pieces, and sometimes the innovative big picture eludes them. The builders are fast movers and make action happen.

The builder mindset to me is kind of the builder, the bricks and mortar, it is putting down the infrastructure and building this sort of permanent or semi-permanent shell around you. I think it is much around the mindset where you need to put your focus [on building] success, and you need to put down some roots and build strong relationships. In order to do that, then you are in it for the long term, so that evokes from me kind of a long-term interdependency; you know a builder is very much dependent on others for success and for sustenance, they require people to take on different roles in order for the community to be successful. A builder would be a methodical thinker, a planner.

– Claire Smith, VP Sales and Marketing,
Vancouver Convention Centre

Potential Avatar of a Builder Mindset

Manager "X" is an energetic, vibrant, fast-talking, A-type personality holding a team meeting to go over the status of projects:
The manager enters the board room where everyone is waiting. It is 8:30 a.m. The manager is late and seems rushed. Manager "X" launches directly into giving congratulations to Joanna on leading her team to success on the Advantage project. The Manager looks around the room and continues to speak:

"You could all learn from her and her team, who have been self-reliant, creative, focused, sticking to the milestones and deadlines, and producing a worthy outcome for the company. However, for the rest of you and your projects, there is much to be desired. This leads me to this update and some decisions I have had to make on the existing projects you are all involved in.

I am being pressured by my bosses on the remaining projects for this quarter, and I need you all to step it up. Over the next two days, I will be reassigning all your positions and will be taking some people off who I feel are under performing—some of you may know already who you are. We can have a conversation one to one on that. I am splitting up Joanna's team and sending them to the other teams to motivate and drive the projects as they have shown the right tenacity and competencies. We all need to up our game if we are going to make the deadlines of this quarter, and that means working long hours, so clear your plate.

I know you can all manifest; it's now urgent to show this. I am not personally going to take the blame on this if you aren't performing; that is your responsibility. I am committed to helping you all go the extra mile, and I will be available from 7 a.m. to midnight to make sure everything is done. If there are any questions, let me know, otherwise I need to meet with my boss. Start upping your game right now. The reorganisation of the teams will be ready by the end of the day. At that time, I will hold another meeting at 7 p.m.—no questions asked. Thanks, and talk to you all later."

Qualities and Characteristics of the Builder Mindset

STRENGTHS

- are the builders of an organisation
- are detailed and big-picture thinkers
- are methodical thinkers
- are A-type personalities
- are fast workers

- are focused, results driven
- are energetic, reliable, committed, hard working
- will adapt to a given vision
- strive to move forwards
- are the typical workforce that makes things happen

- have a tendency to be impatient, bossy, restless
- are competitive
- are petty, blamers, stubborn, skeptics
- can get nasty if something is not going their way
- are perfectionists
- can lean towards being high maintenance.
- are demanding: my way or the highway
- tenacity can lead to burnout
- are okay with doing things that might not be ethical or legal
- can work too fast sometimes

If you have too many builders in your organisation, you might open yourself up to building rapidly but without the sustainability of the settlers to keep it humming. If you have a builder as CEO, innovation or risking new pastures may be challenging, or your corporation may have too narrow a vision. They will often use the bottom line, quarterly returns, and short-term thinking as their guide. On the other hand, if you don't have enough builders, you will struggle to flourish or be competitive as a company. You need a balance of mindsets for different periods of growth and development.

1. When you look at your institution, can you mentally identify who the builders might be? If so, how?
2. In what ways do your builders add value to your organisation?
3. What are some ways you can communicate better with those with a dominant builder mindset typology?

Typology 3: The Nomadic Mindset

Nomads have the mindset of exploring because it is through exploration that you can discover new opportunities, and now with all this transportation, it allows us to explore even further and faster.

– Kwek Kok Kwong, CEO, NTUC
Learning Hub, Singapore

The nomadic mindset is the key focus for this book. Outside of this book, it's the least explored, yet it is growing globally.

The word "nomadic" likely creates images and impressions of what this mindset typology represents. Remember, as Batgerel Bat, Head of Secretariat for Mongolian National Branding Council, stated, "nomad is the movement of the mind."

I would say an internal guiding compass, your mindset, are the principals, the experiences, your frame of references in how you approach various things, so it's very much an internal framework. The nomadic mindset doesn't physically have to be on the move, but I think it's almost like the movement within yourself that you are always moving to the next thing. It might not be a place, but it would be to a new idea [or] to a new concept. I think it is that kind of new, fresh renewal.

– Claire Smith, VP Sales and Marketing,
Vancouver Convention Centre

Even if this is your dominant mindset, remember you have all three mindset typologies motoring within you, rising up to the top, like cream, in different situations. There is a steady flow between the mindsets, yet people are normally more influenced by one of the three more than the others.

It is the 'whisper of the future'—the nomadic mindset is best placed to do this–because there is stillness of listening, I can hear the call, which is very quiet, it is a whisper, it's there, and I need to have the internal stillness; so, stillness is part of the nomadic mindset–[the] capacity to still the mind and listen attentively to what needs to unfold next. [There's] a magical quality to it. [It's] a sensing place—it senses the deeper rivers running in me, it senses the environment, it senses the company, it senses—it is kind of a telepathic communication; I don't need to know how you feel as I feel you in me. It is a different set of competencies.

– Robin Alfred, CEO and Founding Director,
Findhorn Consultancy Service

Potential Avatar of a Nomadic Mindset

Organisation "X" is at a turning point financially. Leader "Y" is taking a moment to reflect upon the fully packed day of meetings, calls, and conversations with different employees:
Sitting looking out their office window on the thirty-second floor, "Y" contemplates and explores, from a wide angle, the new directions the company needs to move towards to stay globally relevant. "Y" has already entertained the ideas of the executive team.

"Y" is curious about each element of the proposed ideas presented earlier and looks at what is further needed to make a decision and whether the idea is bold or innovative enough. Also, "Y" asks if these ideas align with their vision and sustainable perspective over the next five years. "Y" further contemplates how important it is to adapt to new and changing times with speed and agility. And how can "Y" convince everyone to move forwards together?

Leader "Y" decides to leave the office and take a walk through different departments to observe the different teams and question different employees regarding their needs and the company's future direction. "Y" believes simple, clear communications are vital to making a decision and then influencing others to travel the journey together. Leader "Y" returns to their office and makes some clear, intuitive, bold, strategic decisions and calls for a meeting of the executive team, staying open to the potential conflicting conversations.

Qualities and Characteristics of Nomadic Mindset

STRENGTHS

- are visionary, curious, big-picture thinkers
- are aligned with a deeper send of purpose, meaning, and vision
- considers future possibilities, looks for opportunities, takes risks
- are creative, innovative, resilient, strong, eager
- are energetic, independent, interconnected
- are inquisitive with a deep sense of listening
- never settle but pioneer and explore
- are flexible, adaptable, agile
- are bold, brave, courageous
- are focused, strategic, driven

SHADOW SIDE

- lack focus
- are unpredictable
- are too independent
- are lone rangers
- are skeptics
- can get frustrated
- move too fast and leave people behind
- can seem arrogant or aloof at times
- can get anxious
- are flighty, not keen on seeing things through

Which Mindset Do You Want?

The nomadic mindset is the mindset of the future for organisations, governments, and the population at large—a sentiment echoed by 100% of the executives I talked with while writing this book due to the global seismic shift of Industry 4.0 surrounding artificial intelligence, major digital transformations, the gig economy, climate change, Fintech, and many other changes affecting humanity. Many think you now need to begin shifting your mindset away from the comfort and status quo of a settler or a builder mindset towards a nomadic mindset if you are to survive the evolution.

1. When you look at your organisation, can you mentally identify who the nomads might be? If so, how?
2. In what ways do your nomads add value to your institution?
3. What are some ways you can communicate better with those with a dominant nomadic mindset typology?

You Need All Three Mindsets!

If you have a plethora of nomads, the company may not grow or build effectively and strategically. On the other hand, if you have a company without nomads, you may not grow fast, be innovative, or see opportunities clearly. You need all mindset typologies in your organisation and government today. Everyone is important. It is even more crucial now because humanity needs to become more adaptable to the changes in today's world.

Remember what happened to the dinosaurs at the end of the Cretaceous Period. They couldn't adapt to the dramatically changing climatic, environmental, and continental shifts. Is there a distant parallel today? Reflect upon this.

That is why in Part 3, with the awareness of Part 2, you will discover the qualities that most typify a nomadic mindset. You are the self-guide in discovering these qualities I believe are familiar to you. It is up to you whether you believe, behave, and act with the knowledge of them as part of your personal or organisational DNA. The choice is always yours. Let's discover the real meat of *The Nomadic Mindset™, Never Settle . . . for Too Long* together.

○ ○ ○

LEADERSHIP RETHINK

Essential nomadic leadership qualities to embody:

Leadership	Balance	Perspective
Mindset	Organisation	Communication
Nomadic	Dinosaur	Insight
Builder	Framework	Clarity
Settler	Mapping	Evolution

FINAL QUESTIONS

1. What mindset does your organization need more of right now? Why?

2. How can understanding these mindsets help you as a leader?

3. What do you want to do with this information?

RETHINK

PART 3

Discovery

○

"The voyage of discovery is not in seeking new landscapes, but in having new eyes"

– MARCEL PROUST

Deep in the Maasai Mara, the Maasai warrior sees an opportunity, lifts his spear, takes aim, and drives the spear towards the lion. Like the Maasai warrior, you have departed on your journey with some basic tools, and now it is time for to discover some of the golden nuggets, the qualities, and the opportunities to learn that define the nomadic mindset, and may I suggest, the core of your existence as a leader. Enjoy the journey.

Embrace Migration

Mission: to promote migration in your organisation

○

"We are migrating . . . where we were is not where we are . . . we are in an evolving world"

– BENSON KIPOLONKA MUNTERE, MAASAI WARRIOR FROM THE MAASAI MARA, KENYA

Photo by Orgil Batsaikhan

DECEMBER 16, 2017, MAASAI MARA, KENYA

I sit in the lounge of the Mara Simba Lodge opposite my Maasai friend, Benson Muntere. His demeanour mesmerizes me: his upright back; still posture; focused eyes; sincere, intent listening nature; and slow-speaking cadence combined with the deep clarity of his experience as a Maasai warrior.

"We are migrating," Benson says. "Where we were is not where are. In each and every change, we expect the best thing to happen; we always expect to do the best."

Benson is referring to how the Maasai culture is migrating towards becoming more educated by letting go of some of their ancient rituals—such as female circumcision or ear piercing and cutting or removing the centre lower tooth—and changing and adapting to the new realities of the world. These new realities have much to do with government regulations, as well as climate change, which is wreaking havoc with the grazing of their livestock. He says they are becoming more "civilized," and this piqués my interest. For him, becoming more civilized means becoming educated. I suggest nomads are, in many ways, more civilized than educated, "civilized people."

> *It is not the strongest of the species that survives, nor the most intelligent that survives. It is the one most adaptable to change.* 🙴

I reflect for a moment on Benson's words and think about how the baseline of human existence, leaders, and organisations is survival. It is survival that is the basis of all mankind. As Darwin stated, "It is not the strongest of the species that survives, nor the most intelligent that survives. It is the one most adaptable to change." This implies a migration to something new, and migration is movement. Migration is a primary force of nature for not only nomads and animals but also for corporations, products, governments, political leaders . . . everyone.

Can you adapt and migrate freely to new environments, thoughts, ideas, frameworks, and processes, personally or in your institution? If not, what is stopping you?

Animal and Human Migration in the Maasai Mara

In the vast Maasai Mara that leads into the Serengeti in Tanzania, animal migration is a twice-yearly occurrence that is a massive tourist attraction. Curious about what lies behind this animal migration and what might be the metaphor that can be applied to leadership and the movement of the mind, if any, I asked Benson to share his thoughts on the matter. Below I share with you my conversation with Benson, word for word. As you read Benson's words, I invite you to look at the answers with an open, curious nomadic mindset and imagine sitting in the Maasai Mara on the edge of the Talek River, with birds singing and wild animals surrounding you.

KC: *What animals migrate?*

BM: Wildebeest, cattle, zebra, buffalo, elephants, gazelles. One of the most interesting aspects of animals is some of them can sense when the rain is coming and the time to migrate. The elephants can sense which area will have rainfall in the days to come and will move to where there are no lions. In the Mara, they will sense it from a few days to a week [before] and will begin to migrate. The wildebeest and buffalos start to protect their young.

KC: *Is there an animal or group that leads the migration?*

BM: Migration is done by large groups. They will communicate together. For example, for the buffalos and wildebeest, the females understand when to give birth and mate. They will make sounds that it is time to migrate and will do so before the birth. Then, when the young are large enough, they will return.

KC: *Does migration happen continually?*

BM: Twice in a year during birth and rain migrations.

KC: *Do the animals sometimes stop, turn back, or change direction?*

BM: They may change direction as they are chasing the wind and rainfall. If they sense danger, they may change the direction.

KC: *What are the predators of the migrating animals?*

BM: The big cats: lions, hyenas, cheetahs, and leopards.

○

At this point in our conversation, I realise migration is not only geographical, it is a metaphor for what humans are always doing in their minds. We migrate from one creative idea to another, one conversation to another, one topic in an executive meeting to another. We give birth to new concepts, processes, ideas, and opportunities on a continual basis, with a bit of settling peppered in to reap the reward or harvest. And we, too, endure stress along the way from predators, opposing voices, shareholders, or ruthless competitors. These seasonal and situational changes of nature happen to not only animals but also to humans and organisations.

Back to my conversation with Benson . . .

○

KC: *Do the Maasai people migrate?*

BM: In the past, we used to migrate once or twice a year and now we are settled.

KC: *Would you move fast when you migrated?*

BM: We moved according to the natural foot and slowly because we are carrying everything.

KC: *How long in advance would you decide to migrate?*

BM: We have different knowledge [than the animals] because we can see the changes in the far distance. When we would see a lot of black clouds, we would go exploring by sending two or three men of our young warriors out who could move fast and come back fast. They then reported to the elder and he would make the decision to move.

KC: *What if there was resistance from some of the clan, and they didn't want to follow?*

BM: If there was resistance or dangerous factors, different warriors would be sent somewhere in different directions. When they came back and shared with the elder, the elder would compare between the two different explorations then decide what is better for the community. It was democratic. If some didn't want to migrate, a different group formed and they would make a different exploration of their choice. Yes, that happened. We would all meet back at the original location and celebrate together with the slaughter of cattle.

○

My mind is operating on two, parallel tracks: one listening to Benson speak, the other associating his ideas with leadership today.

Imagine having a conversation with your executive team and you are speaking about migrating (moving) in one or more directions on a project or merger, developing new territory, or hiring a new executive. Are you exploring thoroughly different options? Why are you migrating at all? How fast or methodically slow are you moving on this migration, and is everything in place to migrate smoothly? Are there opposing factors stopping you, holding you back, or playing the devil's advocate? Who is making the final decision? Migration is definitely what leadership is about. It is normal and the underlining movement of functioning organizational systems.

Migration Is Movement

The first step in this nomadic mindset quest is knowing you are always migrating from an unknown or known state or place to somewhere or something or someone different. Whether you are exploring or pioneering in Mongolia,

Kenya, or the Sahara Desert (physical migration) or migrating from one creative idea to another, joining the C-suite executive team, or negotiating a merger (metaphorical migration), migration is happening everywhere: physically, mentally, emotionally, and spiritually. Let's discover the migration of the mind.

1. As a leader of an organisation,where are you migrating from and to and why?
2. How does migration, more specifically, relate to your organisation as a quality to attain?

Consider a more global perspective of this word "migration," which means "to move from one part of something to another or change or cause to change from one system to another" (Oxford Dictionary 2003). We are referring here to all movement, including the movement of the mind. What, who, and where is the nomad in your mind?

Are We Ever Not Moving?

As a human being, "you are never not moving." All parts of your physical, mental, emotional, social, and spiritual energies are moving in some way, shape, or form. If you sit in stillness, still you are breathing, and your blood is running through you. As a leader, when you are reflecting you are never not moving in your mind; if you are in an executive team meeting or a client meeting or speaking to your whole company at your annual conference, you are never not moving—everything is in motion, even if it is microscopically slow.

> **As a human being, "you are never not moving."**

Even in meditation, you cannot stop the movement of the mind. However, you can quiet it and just watch the thoughts go by. The mind is like stock market ticker tape, showing the ups and downs of the stock market. This is what is happening in the mind; it is not about stopping it, it is about observing it, not getting involved in the thoughts, just watching and playing witness. Nomads are observers. Are you a leader and observer?

Migration Known as Mobility

Migration is happening all around you, and in organisations it is commonly known as mobility. You have the movement of your people to different geographical locations, migration from one department to another, from one company to another, or movement from one position to another. You have migration of the mind happening in your innovation incubation hubs, with people brainstorming and creating one idea or another. In teams, you have ideas and project targets migrating, and within yourself, you are always migrating from one pasture of ideas, strategies, and tactics to another that align with your vision and direction of the institution.

Is Migration Positive or Negative in Organisations?

Movement or migration can have positive or negative repercussions and implications on your leadership, communication, or strategies. For example, if you move too fast on an innovation launch into a new territory you have not researched or marketed enough, if you have promoted a superstar into an executive position way before they're ready, or if you have migrated a person with the wrong mindset into a place where they do not fit, the outcome is always negative. On the other hand, if you don't migrate in some way, you will be left behind.

With an open mind, explore migration in the different systems and people of your corporation, customers, and partners. These movements are migrations that are an integral component of the nomadic mindset: migration is the movement of the mind.

Arun Madhok, an astute, creative, strategic global thinker and CEO of Suntec Convention Centre in Singapore adds,

> The interesting thing is mobility. Any category of people (mindset) can fluidly move from one to the other. You need to have mobility in every group (mindset). If there is a settler, they must display the acumen to be able to at least move to the next side group (mindset). Because if [they] don't, then they are ready for extinction.

Migrate to Expansion in Organisations

There are four basic reasons for people and animals to migrate physically:

1. to search for food and water
2. to escape natural predators, wars, dictators, politics, or ruthless organisations
3. to find work, a new life and existence, opportunities, and experiences
4. to give birth (mainly animals; however, humans sometimes try to gain citizenship of another country)

> **To survive, you need to be expansive.**

These reasons for migration are directly related to expansion and survival. To survive, you need to be expansive. Expansion of the mind, then, is a vital component of human nature and this is what institutions need to thrive. Expansion is nomadic. Without expansion, you risk becoming redundant or irrelevant.

Often, there is a tendency mentally or physically to obstruct migration or mobility. Robin Lokerman, Group President of MCI-Group in Geneva, Singapore, travels constantly and has developed his company around mobility. He cautions corporations against obstructing mobility:

As soon as you start preventing mobility in an organisation, then you [create] a settler mentality, [and] that's the beginning of the end. So, you need to value your immigration (migration), but you also want to make sure you get the right immigrants.

People living in a different environment than where they were born, and those people I think in the current world, are the most sought after and most successful: those that can live in different environments and adapt and be in other environments, means speaking languages, means speaking and being with different cultures, means building relationships across cultural language borders . . . that's something very important.

Digital Nomads Migrate

When it comes to migration, there is a worthy conversation around digital nomads and millennials. They migrate their businesses to far-off locations, work for digital companies and live up to thousands of kilometres away, or simply work independently. Digital nomads are generally millennials, yet not always, who are freer and want to explore and get away from the gridlock of organisational life. They are expanding their mindsets.

I happened to find Karoli Hindriks through a blog post and consequently had a conversation with her. She is a dynamic, energetic Estonian woman and owner and CEO of an impressive and innovative job placement company called Jobattical. She is working on attaining and introducing the concept of e-visas to governments for digital nomads in a variety of countries. What I found exciting about Karoli is her mindset and the way she sees migration and movement. She says,

Countries are so stuck with their nation status—the agreements that have been here seem to be the only answer. Whereas if you look at the numbers of where the talent shortage is, many countries are suffering from talent shortage, so if you could have an openness, new kinds of agreements would solve their problems.

When we are looking at the mindset, then we should step back. The simplicity of migration has been lost to confusion and complexity of issues, laws, individuals, and processes which are connected to old 'agreements' in the public and private sectors (narrow thinking). Nations are built on agreements that are very static, in other words, people are here, and they will stay here and we will have residency.

Karoli has an expansive mind and is optimistic about the changes appearing globally when it comes to migration and changing these agreements.

When we speak about settling or countries, these are all agreements, which are like a currency. I feel we are on a brink of these agreements being changed. Now we are looking at movement—people are moving around much more, and we are much more independent. I am sitting here, and you are sitting there; it doesn't really matter your nationality. We are in search of new agreements. I believe this is what is creating the tension between people trying to hold onto the agreement *(narrow thinking)* that is already there and another group who is trying to find the new agreements *(expansive thinking)*.

I am sitting here, and you are sitting there; it doesn't really matter your nationality 🙶

On the other hand, in the geopolitical environment, the expansive- (nomadic) versus narrow-thinking (settler and builder) patterns are playing out as multilateralism versus unilateralism on many levels. These are the types of agreements Karoli is referring to. One can only hope we move to nomadic thinking and not continue reverting to settler and builder mindsets.

Karoli has a further thought that reflects the thinking of many millennials today, and it can be a helpful message for organisations and nations to expand their mindsets rapidly.

It is the talent today that chooses where they want to go and live and who they want to work for. As a country, if you are able to adapt to this fact and build a user experience in your country that would basically service these people, you will be the winner.

Are you willing to heed and understand the talent and mindsets of the current and next generations? What if you don't? What are the risks?

As Karoli recognizes,

From an organisational level, companies are beginning to understand this, it is not the CEO who decides who the talent is to join them, rather the talent is choosing the company they want to work with. Employment has already reversed. And the countries have been slower in thinking this.

Today, more than ever, you, as leader, have to be ready, willing, and able to adapt to rapid changes in the workforce. As Karoli says, "it is with the old agreements you make borders, and borders are not only physical, but a large part mental." It is the nomadic mindset that is the most adaptive of the mindset typologies. It is a person who is able to adapt and migrate to new locations, new technologies, new ways of thinking.

it is with the old agreements you make borders, and borders are not only physical, but a large part mental 🙶

1. What is making you or forcing you or your corporation to migrate mentally or physically?
2. What do you need to do to help your employees embrace migration in your organisation (not only physical movement, but mental movement and flexibility)?
3. What are the potential consequences if you put up borders around migration in your organisation?

Mindset as Predator

Combining what I learned from my Maasai friend, Benson Muntere, about migration and the movement of the mind with what I learned from Karoli about old agreements, I've determined your mindset can be a predator.

As animals and nomads migrate, their lives are at risk from all kinds of predators. The most common predators in nature are the big carnivorous cats, other human beings, governments, and corporations. In organisations, migration and the movement of the mind all have risks attached to them, and along the way there can be many predators. They may be competitors, egocentric bosses, competing products, or customers—predators come in all shapes, sizes, and forms.

One of the biggest predators of all is your own thinking or your mindset. The limitations of your mind movement can create a static environment and cause you to settle for the status quo. This is not migrating. Opposing migration goes against the flow of nature. Migration stems from nature, and we humans need to reconnect to this simple fact of life. The migration in your mind will keep you adept and ahead of the pack.

The predators of nature are different than in business; however, as a wise leader, you can recognize the predators of today through your nomadic leadership mindset, and you can seek to adapt rapidly to the intrinsic and extrinsic challenges. It is imperative for your survival on many levels.

Who are the predators in your world?

The Millennial Mindset

A common (and unjustified) complaint over the past five years within organisations has to do with millennials and their way of being and mindset. Millennials have become like a predator for some leaders and human resources departments, but institutions must change their attitudes, behaviours, and mindsets to include, and learn from, this different, vast generation. You have to wake up and migrate your mindset to a more inclusive, nomadic way of thinking and move away from the settler and builder mindsets.

As Karoli says,

> People think that millennials are flakey. Organisations complain about them; however, they can bring to the table different creativity, and with their thinking you need to operate a little bit differently. It is about the contribution that the person will bring to the organisation; that is most important.
>
> We had a guy put down $50,000 to us to show his commitment. This comes back to the modern workforce. People are looking for a purpose and impact and with this they are ready; therefore, people cannot be another line in the PnL [profit and loss]; people are more caring about the why— I believe this is the main reason. If you can't give their work a purpose— help them see the meaning of their work—previously it was I had a job to pay my bills and do the cool stuff, and now it is more I want to do the meaningful stuff, not the cool stuff. The most successful placements wherever they are in the world are the jobs with the meaningfulness and that impact they can leave. I, personally, don't want to waste time on things that don't make a difference.
>
> Organisations fail to acknowledge this type of behaviour. They are not like that; they are not flakey. They actually care more than any other previous generation of workforces.

Millennials are the leaders of the future. They're not burdened by old ways of governing or leading. Even though not all millennials are nomadic, I enjoy being with their youthful, spirited energy; general enthusiasm; and speed with which they use technology. This is vital for the future of work, and we are in the future

> **They're not burdened by old ways of governing or leading.**

now. They are the tech and gig generation and have leapfrogged all the incremental developments leading to technology today. They need a world and corporation that is caring, has a purpose to it, shares, collaborates, and offers institutional learning, and they have a mindset with a high-speed processor. Organisations need to embrace the multigenerations, and this takes communication, understanding, and migrating to expansion.

Be Bold and Migrate

It is time for leaders to migrate, to remove borders, and to not be beholden to rigid quarterly reports and key performance indicators. It is time to adapt to the mindset of the future. Be bold and see migration as not only physical but a constant movement of the mind. Invite the nomad in your mind to wake up. Break down all the borders so you can migrate freely.

I learned a lot during my conversation with my Maasai friend, Benson, about the value of migration as it relates to nature and realised how directly applicable it is to today's leadership. Just as Benson and I finish our conversation, I look into his wise eyes, and he smiles and says,

> We know where we came from, but we don't know where we are going. You can tell what happened in the morning, but you can't tell what the evening will be. You can only tell what happened in the past months, but you cannot tell what the next year will bring.

I say thank you to Benson for his kindness and sharing his knowledge. With deep curiosity, my mind migrates to more questions I want to explore and learn about from him and the other Maasai people. Such richness fills me with joy. I sense a migration of energy within me.

○

This is the art of migration. To migrate fully, there are other qualities you want to explore to help you in your expansion. Your next stop on the journey to *The Nomadic Mindset*™ is for you to Adopt the Anatomy of a Bird.

○ ○ ○

LEADERSHIP RETHINK

Essential nomadic leadership qualities to embody:

Migrate	Sense	Open
Movement	Resilience	Curious
Mind	Speed	Accept
Adapt	Direction	Encourage
Borderless	Freedom	Communication

FINAL QUESTIONS

1. What have you learned about yourself in this chapter?

2. How do you see the concept of migration (movement) now in reference to your life, your organisation, and the world in general?

3. What are some concrete ways you can embrace migration to uplift your corporation?

Adopt the Anatomy of a Bird

Mission: to adopt methods to create stillness, listening, and alertness

○

"When you are out in the in the jungle or roaming the land with your cows, you need to be tuned into stillness and alertness all at the same time—and all of the time"

– JOEL SOIT, MASSAI TEACHER, MASSAI MARA, KENYA

Photo by Essoo Khulan Baljinnyam

DECEMBER 17, 2017, KENYA

Maasai Mara Wake-up

Have you ever woken up to the sweet, scintillating sound of the birds serenading you? The early morning chatter, ever so vibrant and soothing at the same time, greets me this December day. I sense this marvelous rhythm of the day ahead reverberating through me. The sun is beginning to raise its beautiful, bright head, and I feel a great sense of calm as that sun begins to rise inside of me.

Positioned on my balcony overlooking the Talek River, I sit in stillness to meditate. I go deep inside myself and focus on listening to my mantra to distract me from the sounds of the birds. I am also keenly aware of the mischievous monkeys prowling around and climbing onto balconies and sit ready to respond if they approach me. That still space surrounds me, and I gloriously rest there for about thirty minutes before coming out of the rich and calming meditative space.

What comes out of meditation for me is creative thoughts or clear solutions about questions I have not thought of before. In that openness of space and freedom, something arises.

That morning what arises is the image of a bird and how stillness, listening, and alertness are like the anatomy of a bird, a metaphor natural for nomads. The two wings represent stillness and alertness, and the body, listening and the sensing mind. This brings about a calmness radiant in its simplicity.

My vision, when opening my eyes, has the clarity and sharpness of the Talek River and the wooded grasslands of the Mara that stretches out in front of me.

The Anatomy of the Bird

Think about a time you stopped to listen to the birds. To really listen. Have you ever noticed or experienced that moment where all the different sounds created by all kinds of species of birds come together like an organic symphony of nature's true instruments? Within those sounds is silence and stillness. Within those sounds is *Within those sounds is silence and stillness* activity and alertness. And in between those is the listening body, with one ear to stillness and one ear to alertness. The two—stillness and alertness—are like the two wings of a bird. It gives you flight and freedom.

Sometimes, as you venture out on your journey of discovery, you may need to take flight with your ideas, thoughts, and actions, yet you also need to be intentional. This takes a mind that is calm, open, and ready to act at any moment.

As Victor Frankl, Austrian neurologist, psychiatrist, and Holocaust survivor, so eloquently states, "Between stimulus and response, there is a space. In that space lies freedom and power to choose our response. In our response lies our growth and freedom."

The space of freedom, in this case, is the listening body of the bird, and each wing is stimulus and response. The body of the bird is ready and willing at any time to respond to stimulus. Notice the word "respond" and not "react."

Words have energy and weight. How do you feel when you say both those words, and where do you feel them in your body? What happens to your muscles, your heart rate, the movement in your mind?

To me, the word "respond" implies mindfulness, logic, and flexibility. "React" implies aggression, potentially explosive and rigid. To respond implies preconceived thought; to react is to act on instinct, without thought, like the fight-or-flight mechanism in the brain.

In that space lies freedom and power to choose our response 🙶

Sitting in meditation on that balcony, I am ready to respond if a monkey appears on my balcony. In meditation, your senses are heightened and ready for any possibility, even though you are not focusing on anything in particular. You are detached; that is the goal. That sense of deep awareness allows you to know the monkeys are around yet not connect with them. If they approached, I would be able to respond to them in a mindful and detached way.

Freedom through Flight

Sitting and meditating on the balcony in the Mara is like taking flight into space. Freedom!

Have you ever experienced a calm at work, when things are going smoothly and you feel this sense of freedom and oneness with your leadership, and then something happens in an executive team meeting, perhaps you are attacked for making a decision that didn't include another member of your team (or insert your situation here), and you instantly react and fly out of your peaceful state? This can happen many times during the day. How do you get that calm back and respond instead of react?

The answer is in the anatomy of the bird:

- Pause, be still, breathe, listen intently, keep breathing, pause, be alert, and respond from a place of logic.
- Be mindful not to match the volume or intensity of the reaction from others.

I found tremendous silence in the environment of the Maasai Mara, but you don't have to travel around the world to find silence. Take a walk in the woods, or by the sea, or the park, wherever you are. Discover the magic of nature unfolding in front of you, around you, and within you. This is part of the nomadic mindset. It is the nomadic roaming inside your mind and your whole being. Here you can discover that alert stillness as sisters or brothers revealing themselves at different times or at the same time. Meditation, reflection, and journaling all helps!

Stillness as Necessity

There is a Maasai proverb that says, "The forest has ears." This proverb speaks exactly to what I sensed that morning, meditating on the balcony. You've probably heard of the saying, "The walls have ears." It's typically a caution: you never know who is listening, so be careful of your words. The Maasai proverb is similar and yet different. As Joel Soit, a Massai teacher in Massai Mara, Kenya, mentions, "we need to be still enough to be alert and ready to listen to all."

The forest is alive with a cacophony of pleasant, yet distracting, sounds. It is the same in the forest of organisations: negotiations, shareholder meetings, team meetings, project planning, or just the overall buzz in the halls. Being always alert to the sounds allows you to be ready for new possibilities, innovations, and relationships and vigilant of the opposite: the predators or opposing forces.

> **❝we need to be still enough to be alert and ready to listen to all**

In the forest, the animals and birds are listening to, observing, and sensing the potential dangers. You, too, need to be still enough to be alert and ready to listen to your environment, internally and externally. Are you still enough to listen to your forest— the conversations within you, your organisation, or your outer world? Are you alert enough to respond to any new possibilities or approaching predators?

After that balcony meditation, I take a long morning walk on "the Mara" with Joel to his *enkang* (village). He mentions, calmly and nonchalantly, that a lion killed two of his cows last night while they were grazing. Concerned, I ask how his boys (herders) were. "Okay," he says. There is a pause in the conversation, and I realise this is a simple fact of life for him. Stuff happens. Our conversation fluidly changes direction, and we move on just like the nomads do; they don't dwell on things, and they move on quickly from one situation to another. Joel and I continue our long walk on the Mara.

"Why is it the nomads appear to be still and yet so alert at the same time?" I ask him. Joel, majestic and dignified in his checkered Maasai dress, jewellery, club, and walking stick, calmly looks at me with his wise eyes, then turns and looks over the land.

Why is it the nomads appear to be still and yet so alert at the same time? 〝

Joel explains that life in the Mara is about survival, and one needs to be still and alert, always listening to ensure survival.

> We don't dwell on it, yet we face the environment every moment of our life. It's just us. We are interconnected. Our cows are the most important parts of our lives, and our lives surround the survival of our cows. They are our currency. We need to protect them and treat them well by finding land to graze so they become big and healthy. We need to send them out to graze, and nature is clear, raw, and unrelenting. We cannot control nature and how it will respond.

I nod and Joel continues:

> As Maasai, we need to stay very still inside and outside while we herd our cattle, be observant, and listen with our eyes, ears, heart, and intuition and get curious of every little sound or movement that is around. That stillness is vital to live, and the alertness you need to have when an approaching lion appears, watches, and attacks. Then you need to make fast decisions. Sometimes you are too late, and the lion has got your cow, yet you need to be calm and still in your alertness to protect the rest of the herd, yourself, and your community.
>
> From a very early age, we learn to respect the nature and the environment we live in. We are one with the animals, the weather, the land, the environment. We are one with our people. We are interconnected. To sustain our land, animals, family, community; stillness, listening, and alertness are a major part of our existence in surviving the harsh reality of our lives.

Have We Diverted from These Qualities?

That got me to thinking, are these qualities (stillness, listening, alertness) of the nomadic mindset something we have lost over the centuries, or do we still observe them but in a different way? What are the most important parts of our lives and businesses (our "cows")? What threatens them (our "lions")? How can you, by staying still, become more observant?

I believe some may consciously, or unconsciously, heed these qualities; however today, because people live so far outside themselves in their busy lives or businesses, they have lost these skills in many ways. In an organisational setting, this can lead to burnout, stress, and lack of motivation, which leads to decreased performance or effectiveness or disengagement. Because of these maladies, companies have been driven to find interventions to alleviate these maladies. They pay for mindfulness, meditation, well-being, and deep-listening workshops to reawaken what was sleeping inside us.

Even though these are great interventions, they may not be treating the cause of the problem. Some companies are listening and making systemic changes in working situations such as flextime, telecommuting, environmental architectural design changes, smaller autonomous teams, and more. This is fantastic. It takes real initiative from the leader to take on the anatomy of a bird and figure out the underlying systemic problems, and then responding accordingly. Ignoring the Anatomy of a Bird will not work if you ignore the cause(s), especially with the new workforce.

Listening, Stillness, and Alertness as Leadership Qualities

Stillness, listening, and alertness are fundamental leadership qualities and will help you, your teams, and your institutions find the true essence of how to be successful as you move forwards in this fast-paced, disruptive world. Today, you and your corporation are being swallowed up by the data transformation tsunami, and this is where these qualities are vital to help you maintain your sanity and well-being. An unwell leader is not an asset. These three qualities are drivers of the nomadic mindset, and they can help slow you down in moments of increased speed.

A leader needs to be bold enough to balance belief in their vision and people with heading off the potential opposing voices of the forest (shareholders, Wall Street, or hostile executives or partners). This sometimes means disrupting the status quo.

Linda Georgina Locke, a Brand Consultant in Singapore, says,

> We need to go away and explore new territory, and I think we need someone to assist in this. Nomadic thinking is what we need; then step out and give yourself time to find a way to be a nomad again. You need someone in the company who knows when to use the sledgehammer. This is disruption.

In many ways, moving to a nomadic mindset *is* disruption. Especially for those who do not recognize these qualities, or if they do, do not exhibit them in their daily managerial or leadership behaviours or technical functions within their organisation.

It is the function of the leader to listen, contemplate, and observe what is happening and stay alert to disruption and environmental noise and use that sledgehammer appropriately, like a spear of a Maasai, to get things done. But you need to be still and alert and listen intently to the symphonic vibrations in your environment with the freedom of the nomadic mindset.

Follow Through with These Qualities

On the other hand, Linda reflects that she has worked with leaders who, while claiming they understand needing a "time out" to refresh, do not follow through. This is poor leadership.

She feels that "listening skills and having the genuine desire to listen . . . must come from the top." However, she also says that,

> Often, somewhere in the organisation, all this knowledge and understanding goes nowhere. There are people who have some great ideas, and you are losing out because you don't listen. You need to harness this; otherwise, it is a lose-lose situation. You need to listen.

What she always felt was beneficial in solving this situation was sharing sessions in an open environment where you can solve the problem. This energizes people.

Is this you? Do you know of leaders like this?

Sorting out the cacophony of sounds in today's global, diverse forest environments takes a nomadic, still, alert mindset with a strong team of nomadic, builder, and settler mindsets to traverse the digital transformation information movement.

Here is an example. Corporations buy into the belief that they need all this expensive technology, some of which is useful and some is not. Sales people often sell companies too much expensive technology, and then the institution doesn't have the knowledge or capability to manage it. To prepare for the future, you need to be open enough to be still and alert and listen to what you truly need to determine what is truly tied to the success of the corporation at every milestone, without getting stuck in "the bottom line."

Disconnected Society versus Interconnected Society

Today, people in general are not still enough to listen intently and be alert at the same time. It is a growing complaint that people are disconnected from each other and only connected to technology. Preoccupation with texting, Whatsapping, Facebooking, games, or other media diminishes stillness and our listening skills and alertness to danger when walking on the sidewalk, across the street, or in the office. Why? Because you are in your own world and not connected to the outer world. Hence, what is missing is not connection but the understanding of the interconnection of things.

When I was living in New York City, someone told me I'd develop a sixth sense, a deep intuition. It was about survival and safety. I remember I did develop my stillness, alertness, and listening skills in a different way than my previous environment demanded. If I was walking outside, I was alerted to respond when I heard someone running behind me, just as a nomad living in the Mara would have. I was alert to all things at all times: voices, speed, volume, noises, proximity, environment, etc. This requires being still and alert and listening all at the same time. When did you last take notice of these qualities?

I was alert to all things at all times: voices, speed, volume, noises, proximity, environment, etc. 🟠

Compare this state of interconnectivity to when one is walking and looking down at their phone—texting, reading, or watching videos. You are cut off from the environment around you, only connected to the phone and not interconnected to everything around you. This can be dangerous. Generally, this interconnection is lost today (Ironically, some of those walking while on their phones might be reading articles and social media posts on this very topic!).

These qualities—stillness, alertness, and listening—live within everyone, affecting you and your company as a whole ecosystem. It is a way of being. What would adopting these nomadic qualities of the Anatomy of a Bird mean for your leadership and your organisation? How can they make your corporation more efficient, productive, and sustainable?

How to Develop the Anatomy of a Bird

If it seems maybe there isn't any hope, remember, there always is an alternative choice, and hope lives there. Developing the Anatomy of a Bird will help make you a more wise, astute, and complete leader who can migrate on many levels much more fluidly and effectively. Think of developing this anatomy as developing a muscle. To develop and grow a muscle, you need to exert stress upon the muscle itself, i.e., train it by adding extra weight or more repetitions. It takes practice. Perhaps think of developing the Anatomy of a Bird as developing the intuition muscle, gut feeling, or sixth sense. Developing it isn't hard, and there are many ways to do so. Here are a few ways:

1. Slow down and keep your senses open and free to whatever is surrounding you or on the horizon.
2. Take time to reflect or meditate. If you are new to meditation, I recommend looking into meditation recordings or apps. Listen to podcasts or online courses on meditation. Start by sitting and focusing on your breath for five minutes, and then keep extending the time slowly. Find a quiet place to sit, or take a silent walk, or look outside a window at nature.
3. Take walks in nature and consciously speak to yourself: *what I see is . . . what I hear is . . . what I feel is. . . .* During your walk, stop every so often, take a deep breath, then do a slow, 360-degree turn, scanning all you can before pausing and moving on with your walk, listening to all sounds, movements, colours. . . .
4. You can also take yourself, alone, on a city walk during bustling peak times, or sit on the metro or in your car driving home, and take time to observe all movement in your sight range (without staring at someone), listening to all sounds, internal and external.
5. Be still so you can be alert by finding times in the day where you are silent, and then use your senses to observe objects, people, buildings, and your environment.
6. Become completely curious. Ask open questions.
7. In meetings, practice focusing on your breathing when times get rough, when you're unsure of an answer, or when you set the environmental energy of the room.
8. Turn off your devices and technology. Take a technology-free day.

Staying Alert of Predators

Joel, my friend and Massai teacher in Massai Mara says the predators make the Maasai more aware, and that by living side by side with them, you get to understand their movements, intentions, and existence. The king of the jungle, the lion, is a force to be reckoned with, and yet knowing and understanding its habits, behaviours, inner intentions, movements, and locations allows you survive and thrive more freely. As Nelson Mandela once said, "keep your enemy close by."

By adopting the practice of the Anatomy of a Bird, you are more aware and better equipped to courageously face whatever or whoever your predator is. How do you sense who your predators are? What is your natural pattern when dealing with predator situations? How did you respond or react or assert yourself the last time you were confronted?

Arun Madhok, the CEO of Suntec Convention Centre, summarises the Anatomy of a Bird succinctly,

> A nomad is a seeker, always looking over the plate saying, 'What else is there?' I think the nomads are always trying to figure out what the other guy is doing, what's happening around the wall—or around the corner.

This I found to be true with all the nomadic cultures I visited. When you observe them walking, sitting, eating, chatting, marketing, trading, or herding, their stillness is profound, yet you know there is a depth of listening and alertness humming like a symphony inside them, ready to crescendo in a split second. What will it take for you to revisit these nomadic qualities?

○

During our walk, Joel takes me to visit Mary, his mother, in her dung hut. We sit, speaking from time to time, while I watch the children play. I listen to the sound of the wind and reflect on how Mary also embodies the Anatomy of Bird.

○

And now it's time to migrate to the next golden nomadic quality: possessing the Eyes of a Hawk . . . but before you move on, I invite you to take one last look at a summary of this very important leadership day . . .

○ ○ ○

build your bird from the inside out

inside of you is a deep instinctive natural intuition
that has survived the test of time
and it lives in
the anatomy of a bird.

the nomad in you knows this,
as
it is part of your nomadic DNA.

it may be sleeping inside of you
waiting, wishing and hoping
you will listen deeply to
its voice saying,
be still in the symphony of life,
be alert to the symphony of life
and
sense what this might be
by getting curious, intently curious.

tap into the free interconnected you
by spreading your expansive wings,
stand tall in your body
and
be present,
by
adopting the anatomy of the bird:
listen : stillness : alertness

LEADERSHIP RETHINK

Essential nomadic leadership qualities to embody:

Awareness	Freedom	Anatomy
Stillness	Stimulus	Practice
Listening	Respond	Muscle
Alertness	Mindfulness	Adopt
Curious	Reflect	Adapt
Open	Observe	Intuition

FINAL QUESTIONS

1. Do you take time to be still? To reflect? If so, how? If not, how can you add stillness to your daily life?

2. What are some interventions and practices you can enact in your institution to improve deep listening?

3. What are some benefits to you if you practiced these qualities?

Possess the Eyes of a Hawk

Mission: to keenly develop your vision

○

*"The only think worse than being blind
is having sight but no vision'"*
– HELEN KELLER

DECEMBER 18, 2017, MAASAI MARA NATIONAL RESERVE, KENYA

Today is another great opportunity to understand nature and nomads. I rise early at the Mara Simba Lodge in Maasai Mara, Kenya. It's time to head off on a safari in the great Maasai Mara National Reserve, which borders the Serengeti in Tanzania.

After breakfast and gathering cameras, tripod, different clothes for the rising temperature, and a picnic lunch, I meet Saruni, my safari guide, and Joel Soit, the Maasai teacher. Saruni, an entrepreneurial guy like many Maasai, has a Land Rover he rents from a fellow Maasai brother in the community. Community and sharing is everything here: it equals solidarity and assists in your survival. Joel and Saruni, dressed in their traditional Maasai clothing and jewellery, and I head off along the bumpy roads to the reserve.

We drive through the National Reserve, sticking to the well-worn, gravel roads while witnessing a variety of wild animals living and eating nearby. We see giraffes, baboons, zebras, ostriches, gazelles, wildebeests, elephants, and more, all living in harmony doing their own thing while sticking with their families and tribes, so to speak. It is breathtaking, and the stillness in the air is gratifyingly meditative. Joel and Saruni speak from time to time in hushed voices; I sit in awed silence. The birds speak to each other, and the animals silently go about their grazing, oblivious to potential intruders (like us tourists).

It is breathtaking, and the stillness in the air is gratifyingly meditative. 🙶

We stop along the way to take pictures, and it is during one of these stops I observe the Eyes of a Hawk Saruni and Joel innately possess as they scan the horizon. It is stillness in action.

The air is soft against the skin, like a gentle buoyancy keeping me afloat. I feel as though I'm in a National Geographic documentary experiencing the real sights and sounds of nature at its best. The "Circle of Life" from The Lion King resonates in my ears . . . I am living the vision, the dream I have wanted for years, experiencing it alongside two wonderful Maasai.

Saruni is on his walkie-talkie, asking other drivers of any "Big Five" (lions, leopards, rhinos, elephants, or hippos) sightings.

"Look over there," Joel points. I look but cannot see what he's pointing at. This happens again and again, with Joel and Saruni pointing to things they see but I cannot. I need binoculars to scan the horizon and recognize what they are seeing, still I see with difficulty. I am amazed at the visionary ability of Saruni and Joel, at how they can see an animal moving in the grasslands—behind or between bushes—and how they can even see the small interactions between different animals sometimes a kilometre away.

The parallel track in my mind wonders how this can relate to leadership.

Leadership Vision

Obviously, having a powerful vision and creating a vision for an institution is paramount for a leader. However, it doesn't always exist or exists only in part. Whether you are in the expansive grasslands of Mongolia, the desert of the Sahara, the wilderness of Kenya, or the expanse of your industry, vision is vital. Vision is linked directly to survival and success in life. The leader needs to see all the movements forwards, possibilities, opportunities, threats, and risks plus recognize the potential of their business model from a nomadic mindset. Many factors go into creating the vision of an organisation.

Seeing—whether long or short distances—with clarity of mind is exactly what you need to do. It is also your duty to hire and train others to have both long- and short-range vision so they can see, observe, and make clear decisions with the speed of a cheetah, even if—and especially if—your world has become too quarterly focused.

Meanwhile . . .

All of a sudden, Saruni gets a message that two cheetahs are patiently eyeing an impala (a type of antelope) on the grasslands. Off we go, Saruni driving like another Formula 1 driver, heading in what seems to me random directions over the vast, rolling terrain towards the targeted spot. As we approach the area, we see many other 4×4s converging from all directions. Slowing down, we creep as close as we can to the cheetahs. We stop and turn the engine off. The only sounds you can hear are the voices on the walkie-talkies.

> **The only sounds you can hear are the voices on the walkie-talkies.**

Then Saruni, calmly and without raising his voice, says, "There they are: a mother and her son." He says, "The son must be almost ready to leave his mother."

We sit and watch patiently. In plain view, the mother has her eye on an impala about two hundred metres away behind some bushes. The Impala emerges from the bushes, seemingly oblivious to its fate. It is magic to watch the cheetahs move with such intense focus on their target. They move stealthily, stalking their prey with total disregard for the eight 4×4s full of gawking tourists watching this real and raw performance.

The cheetahs' target, the impala, appears to be oblivious—a parallel situation that can also play out in aggressive company take-overs; when leaders, managers, or partners do not share information; or when an institution moves slowly and strategically into new territory. Be careful of being sideswiped by another. Be a conscious observer and move as a stealthy cheetah, always alert. Are you a cheetah or an impala? Do you sometimes play both roles?

Between the cheetahs and the impala is a shallow ravine and a dried-up river. The two cheetahs stand still, then regally sit down and look in different directions as if maybe there is another, easier target somewhere else. Then all of a sudden, the mother starts to move, but faster this time, towards her original prey. All the 4×4s start their engines and race to the other side of the ravine, being careful not to alert the impala or the cheetahs. We all take up a position opposite of the cheetahs' direction. The tension builds. We stop and wait patiently, quietly watching, with binoculars, the impending kill.

> **As the cheetahs move closer and closer to their prey, you can see them crouch lower, ready to attack**

As the cheetahs move closer and closer to their prey, you can see them crouch lower, ready to attack. Then, with the impala in sight, the turbo-charged cheetahs take off at lightning speed towards the impala, and *pounce*! They land a direct hit on the impala's neck. The mother attacks while the son watches. She pulls the impala down; it struggles and tries to get away, then almost does, but both cheetahs pull it down and hold onto its neck until it stops moving.

I feel a bit of sadness for the impala. However, on a more practical note, I revert to a corporate mindset and realise this is a metaphor for human nature. Corporate, institutional, and philanthropic processes and systems often mirror the processes, strategies, and tactics exhibited in nature. Both animals had the same goals: survival. We cannot judge the cheetah for wishing to eat what it naturally is meant to eat.

What similarities does your corporation share with this account of the cheetah and the impala?

After this excitement, we wander the Mara further till we stop to have our lunch at the Mara River, which divides Kenya and Tanzania. The low riverbed below us allows a full herd of gazelles to migrate unimpeded. It's enlightening to observe the still, calm movement of the leader as he stands in the front, then at the back, and then at the side, always on guard and alert, ready to respond to predators. Nature teaches us the true values and rules of life and of an institution at it most basic level. This is how great leaders see and care for their "herds," "tribes," teams, and individual employees as well as clients. They keep an eye on them while letting them be free.

1. How does this nature metaphor reflect your visionary leadership?
2. Do you protect, move around the halls of your organisation, or watch over the territory for your people?
3. If so, how and what would you like to improve upon?

The Agility of the Cheetah in Leadership

A leader needs to keep a clear forwards direction using the strategies and tactics in place while being aware of any external opportunities or threats that could happen at any time, throwing you off course. This is when agile thinking and resilience is paramount.

This is when agile thinking and resilience is paramount 🙰

The cheetah sees what it wants, and while it may consider changing directions, it bounces back and goes after it with intense focus. Joel and Saruni, too, were agile and resilient as they were sharp, quick thinkers, never giving up on finding various experiences. In a way, they mirrored the calm, slow, patient nature of the cheetah: when it was time to act, they pounced.

Are you, your company, and your employees agile and resilient like the cheetah while still possessing the Eyes of a Hawk?

Creating the Vision

It is usually the CEO who creates and develops the vision or direction of an organisation, with input from their executive team or board of directors. This vision-making is a nomadic mindset quality. Once the vision is clearly defined and shared, it is followed by developing (builder mindset) the strategy and tactics needed to achieve success. This process is followed by the glue of the corporation watching over and fulfilling everything that keeps the company moving towards the vision (settler mindset). All three of these mindsets are working together in an interconnected way through processes and systems—at least that is the hope.

When Mads Winblad, a consultant and former Nokia executive, works with start-ups, he asks for the company's vision. He says that, more often than not, people are not on the same page when it comes to vision:

One says something, another says something, and you figure out that they are not aligned at all. My point is, if they don't have an understanding or vision for themselves, for the company, everything else, then it won't work. You need to be concrete about what you want and how you want to look like in these years.

The mother cheetah had a strong vision; Saruni and Joel also had a strong vision. They all saw an opportunity by assessing their surroundings, then migrated towards the goal: for the cheetah, food for herself and her young son, for Saruni and Joel, giving me the fulfilling experience for which they were paid. These examples were goals or targets, yet there needs to be vision—a compelling reason to align and come together around a large or small objective and direction.

> **❝ What I found interesting during our conversation was this relationship of the Eyes of a Hawk**

What are some practices you can put in place now and later to start focusing on your vision, purpose, and mission?

One way of creating organisational agility and resilience is to spot and develop your talent—the talent that is going to drive your corporation towards your vision. Think like a nomad or a cheetah and think expansively by developing a vision that stimulates creating a robust talent development system. This can be achieved by not only observing peoples' skills, but also by understanding their dominant mindset: nomadic, builder, or settler.

While I was working in India, I met with Vikram Sharma, a humble man with a vibrant mind and smile. He is the General Manager and Head of Human Resources at Tata Motors Passenger Vehicles, Tata Motors, India. What I found interesting during our conversation was this relationship of the Eyes of a Hawk—vision—with that of the cheetah and the nomadic mindset in relation to Tata. Tata is a good example of how this quality works, specifically, in the area of leadership talent selection.

Talent Development Case Study: The Tata Group

Vikram's statement reflects the intention of the cheetah:

> Whenever the leaders of Tata see an opportunity, they see it with a hawk's eye, evaluate it, and then they move at the right, appropriate time, so if they see that a sector has a value proposition and is worth investing a few

billion dollars, they want to have a piece of that pie. I would say that is a very sophisticated form of the nomadic mindset.

The Tata Group is one of the oldest legacy organisations left in the world today (Wikipedia 2019). In 1868 India, under British occupation, Jamshedji Tata, the "father of Indian Industrialization," founded the Tata Group, focusing on the steel industry. A hundred and fifty years later, The Tata Group is a major global player in a variety of industrial sectors, such as steel, beverages, hotel chains, technology, consultancy, airlines, commercial and passenger vehicles, communications, chemicals, and retail, to name a few. It is a massive company that continues to move forwards, like a nomad, forging new territories with the Eyes of a Hawk, always seeking opportunities. One of its primary realizations and beliefs since its inception is to give back to society. Why? Because as Jamshedji says, "Business cannot survive in a society that is failing."

Business cannot survive in a society that is failing 〞

The first Prime Minister of India, Jawaharlal Nehru, said of Jamsetji Tata (Wikipedia 2019),

> When you have to give the lead in action, in ideas—a lead which does not fit in with the very climate of opinion—that is true courage, physical or mental or spiritual, call it what you like, and it is this type of courage and vision that Jamsetji Tata showed.

Vikram Sharma began working for Tata in 2013. He shares my curiosity about the different mindset typologies and how they relate to business.

> This whole attribute of leadership and nomadic mindset is very carefully nurtured. How it is done is by letting their managers and leaders, at certain levels, take risks, and even if there are failures, there are lessons learned along the way. In fact, this is one company, Tata, I have seen that encourages people to fail, and that is why people have gone forwards, even in very routine innovations or changes in the systems.

Encouragement to fail? This way of thinking certainly builds the agility and resilience of a nomad, qualities important for leaders and future leaders alike.

Speaking of future leaders, the process of selection for upcoming leaders at Tata is quite a lengthy, thorough, deep process. Much like Saruni's and the cheetah's vision, it focuses long and wide at first and then narrows. It is also as Binderiya, my student friend at the National University of Mongolia says, "Think vastly; act narrowly." Vikram explains,

> We have a deeply entrenched advancement scheme and [act] very early to identify these nomads, and then they groom and develop them through agile systems. Through the fast-track selection system every year, the HR comes up with a system and offers it to the people [with] four to six years in the company in [the] age group twenty-seven to thirty-two. Those are employees who have been having top-rated performances and [giving] excellent and strong contribution[s].
>
> They first apply, then take an online filtration exam, and then, for example, out of two thousand applicants, less than two hundred will be shortlisted. They will then go to the assessment centre, have interviews with the board, and following that, about ten or fifteen will be selected. There is a fine development intervention where in 'Leadership One,' they will be nurtured (mentored) for a year by going into different roles to develop multifaceted individuals. Throughout their career, they are then tracked, and these are eventually the nomads for the organisations.
>
> For those not chosen, there are different recognition programs in the company as well. What this does, at Tata, is help in promoting solid citizens who come on time, go on time, and Tata will create an ecosystem, so that they work well and contribute well.

Talent recognition is about mindset. Having the right mindset to first develop a robust recognition system and then identify the right mindset typology needed for specific positions to allow for growth and advancement on different levels will assist in the survival and growth of your organisation. There are more pluses than minuses concerning your return on investment of multiple resources, from human to financial. It is the best investment you can make. It is honouring human talent. The Tata system is just one of many corporations doing the right thing.

1. What if you encouraged failure, leading to better agility and stronger resilience? What would this do for your organisation's performance and success?
2. What if you had a broader vision for talent management? What would that do for your company?
3. What new ways or processes can human resources institute to develop better leaders to possess the Eyes of a Hawk and a nomadic mindset?

Sharing Knowledge

What did the mother cheetah and Saruni do? The cheetah shared the impala with her son; Saruni shared his knowledge with me. Tata shares wisdom internally by developing the next generation of leaders as well as by giving back to groups with the community.

When it comes to giving back, Vikram spoke passionately about Tata's corporate social responsibility (CSR) attitude and it certainly appears to be very rich indeed.

> The reason for what we are doing is for the larger good of society. The founding father of Tata's had this spirit of giving back to society, and it has been institutionalized in the ethos of Tata's. In fact, this philanthropic/ CSR attitude has been well documented and highly regarded in business leadership in India and internationally. We feel we can keep the money to ourselves or give it back to them. The Tatas believe in the act of giving, which leads to personal growth and community development.

Often, Tata would go into remote and far-off areas such as jungles or forest where the people had very little staples of life, i.e., education, clean running water, electricity, enough food, [few] trees, and more. When they would go into these locations, they intentionally would provide [for] and develop the community as well as give them work. Their thinking is that if they are drawing resources from this environment, then it is important to give back to the ecosystem. This helps to develop the individuals and make their lives better. This is the measurement that we want to be remembered by, and this is correlated back to the leadership nomadic mindset.

There are multiple ways of sharing in life and within organisations. Sharing is a component of the Eyes of a Hawk as the hawk can see from above all that is going on below. It is about putting humanity first, and that can be best accomplished by walking your talk; communicating authentically; and seeing, hearing (listening), and understanding others internally and externally.

Sharing benefits productivity; builds trusting, strong relationships, partnerships, and communities; and reflects on performance and engagement. If this is part of the vision of a leader or the Eyes of a Hawk, which it ought to be, then your job is to make sure it cascades downwards—fully.

Cultivating a sharing culture with a focus on CSR shows you care about your world, both internally and externally to your organisation. You must mean it, though. Talent, as Karoli Hindriks of Jobbatical in Estonia says in Discovery, Day 1, is looking at your company and your CSR initiatives to see if they work for you. Today, more than ever, you cannot avoid sharing with a strong visionary intention; it is crucial to the survival of a great and successful institution. Think like a cheetah—the fastest animal alive—with incredible vision, intent, focus, and speed.

What is one thing you can do today to inspire and stimulate a sharing environment?

Possessing the Eyes of a Hawk Is Vital for Organisational Success

Nomads do not roam simply for the reason of moving. They move with a purpose, vision, and a strategy. They always know that there is a reason behind it all.

– Joel Soit

Since the beginning of time, nomads all over the world have understood the importance of possessing the Eyes of a Hawk, of having vision and purpose way before it became vogue and trendy for leadership gurus and business schools. Possessing the Eyes of a Hawk is vital for the potential success of any corporation, and yet it is so often disregarded or misinterpreted. This quality will also develop your expansive thinking, so you can see wider and longer before focusing in on your target.

Do you have the Eyes of a Hawk? If not, what do you need to do to develop your vision?

○

After experiencing the richness of a safari and realising the metaphors and mirrors it represents in life and leadership, we all head back to the Mara Simba Lodge. I give my gratitude to Saruni and Joel and head to my room and sit on my balcony overlooking the vast Maasai Mara to reflect further on the day.

○

Now that you have a greater clarity of vision, you can put this into action like the cheetah and Follow the Rain.

○ ○ ○

LEADERSHIP RETHINK

Essential nomadic leadership qualities to embody:

Vision	Eyes of a Hawk	Observe
Purpose	Strategy	Growth
Giving back	Mindset	Knowledge
Drive	Agile	Leadership
Focus	Resilience	Persistence
Interconnection	Sharing	Alignment

FINAL QUESTIONS

1. How important to you is creating a strong vision?

2. In what ways can you begin to intentionally develop your Eyes of a Hawk?

3. After reading this chapter, what changes do you want to make to your vision by viewing it through the Eyes of a Hawk and remembering the dynamic agility of a cheetah?

RETHINK

Follow the Rain

Mission: to hone your intuition, allowing you to see new pastures ahead

○

"If you are a good hunter, never stay at home.

*Get out; find the tracks of animals;
see where they are going,*

*When they passed through, the wind direction, where to
move, where the grass is tall enough to hide. Then you
will be a good hunter"*

– BUSHMEN ELDER

Photo by Hicham Zemmer

JUNE 10, 2017, GRAND MOSQUE OF PARIS, FRANCE

I sit with Romain Simenel, a French anthropologist who specializes in Berber nomads, sipping a traditional Moroccan mint tea at the Grand Mosque café. Romain is a fascinating and enthusiastic "true nomad" who has spent years researching, travelling, and living with the Berbers in Morocco. I'm excited to have the opportunity to ask him many questions.

"Why do nomads move from place to place?" I ask.

"To follow the rain," he replies.

I'd heard this, or similar statements, before from the Massai and Mongolian nomads, but I am curious to hear Romain's perspective.

> **where am I going to find some grass today for my camels?**

You are under the tent, okay? And you go to bed very early because this is the way in the desert, maybe it's 7:00 or 8:00 p.m. You will wake up early with ease. And then, in the early morning, you climb to the highest point of the desert. Maybe it's a dune or a little mountain or anything high. From here you are going to see the climate; you will observe the birds; you will observe everything. You think: 'where is the place that is more humid?' [and] 'where am I going to find some grass today for my camels?' You want to go and explore, yet sometimes the rain is not in your country.

In the Sahara, sometimes there are only three drops of rain now, and you wait another three months and no rain, then you wait another three months, and you get a few more drops. It's not homogenous; it's not equal. When you are on caravan out in the desert with your family, you may meet someone. It's quite rare, but when you meet someone, the first question, after 'Hello, how are you? How is the family? How are the camels and everything else,' and finally you hear, 'where's the rain?'

Fascinating indeed.

Even though Follow the Rain implies primarily a physical movement, I invite you to view this philosophy from the point of view of mindset and the movement of your mind. The rain could be a new market, trend, product, position, location, creative idea, conversation, intention, or your intuition. It is about following the rain from different angles and perceptions. Doing so will help you see and experience a more holistic nomadic mindset.

Are you ready to follow that rain when it appears?

What does Follow the Rain Mean to a Nomad?

This literal statement is linked to survival. Looking at survival from a nomad's perspective, if there is no rain, then the pastures or grasslands dry up, and if the pastures are barren, then there is no food for their livestock to graze upon. And if the animals cannot eat enough, they will become weak, malnourished, skinny, and will lose all their fat and maybe not survive. Or, they will be worthless, and the nomads won't be able to sell them. If the animals do not survive, neither will the people.

The rain is a major part of nature's food chain. It is as simple as that.

1. What does your food chain look like in your organisation?
2. What happens when your ideas dry up?
3. How do you keep the food chain moving towards the rain and get people to follow?

How do the Nomads Know when the Rain Will Come?

Whomever I spoke to, I would invariably ask, "When do you know the rain is coming or how long in advance do you know when the rain will appear?" They all said they know a week in advance. I was stunned . . . a week in advance? I asked if they listened to the weather reports. They said "No, they watched the animals."

When do you know the rain is coming or how long in advance do you know when the rain will appear?

Animals are the biggest indicators of change in the environment because they have a hyper-sensitivity to unforeseen changes. When they sense a change, they act and behave differently. During the Indonesian Tsunami in 2004, animals started to move to higher ground even before the earthquake and the subsequent tsunami that followed. Observing, like vision, is one of the qualities of Follow the Rain.

Therefore, the reason nomads will move to new pastures or grasslands is purely strategic. They move first to survive, and then to thrive in greener pastures. While on the move, if they find the weather is changing directions, then they will course correct towards the rain. They have to choose whether to stay and possibly miss the rain, which may mean not having food or animals to feed their family and community, or to go, which brings risks such as predators—that might damage their livestock—or the rain not appearing, then they have invested time and energy into a move that wasn't worth it.

Whether sitting on intricately woven carpets and cushions with Habib in his makeshift tent at the Casbah Museum in Tighmert, Morocco, or out on the Sahara in a tent with Mohamed, my Moroccan driver, speaking about the indicators of rain, they all described animals' reactions the same way: dogs roll around in the sand, birds fly in groups, goats shake, camels cry out, and ants move in all different directions instead of following each other in a straight line.

Of all of these indicators, I learned ants are the biggest indicator, as they show an extreme change in behaviour by moving in all different directions as if their GPS system has malfunctioned. As the ants do, through nature's innate intuition and the nomad's interconnectedness with nature, the nomads are able to holistically plan and strategize.

The nomads know where there is rain, there will be plenty of growth in that pasture to harvest, and the animals can graze for a bit longer, and everyone will be happy.

1. What are some forewarning signals that change or disruption is coming to your corporation or industry? What signals might be appearing right now?
2. How trusting of your innate intuition are you? Are you aware enough to observe your corporate environment's mindset?
3. What do you need to do to become more observant as you Follow the Rain, not only of yourself, but of others and situations around you?

Being Light and Nimble

Think very fast and do not to waste your time. Emergencies happen, and you need to find a solution very fast. Elders are thinking very fast.
– Simon Soitanae, Maasai, Head Waiter at the Mara Simba Lodge

When the Maasai decide to migrate, the elders send out their fastest and most strategic warriors to look for the rain and find new pastures. When they return with news, then the elder decides when to move. Nomads need to be light and nimble and ready to move at any time. In Mongolia and Morocco, they can pack up their yurts or tents in twenty minutes, then load up the donkeys, camels, and—now—trucks and motorbikes with all their belongings. They have few possessions and then only what they essentially need. No more no less.

To be light, nimble, and fast refers to not only physically moving your location, but also to being mentally light, nimble, and fast. This means you cannot be weighed down by physical possessions. Keep only what you need to live. Nor can you be weighed down by negative thought patterns, habits, borders, or challenging situations. You need to keep it simple, clear, and to the point. This is the lightness of being the nomads refer to in their lives no matter where I travelled on this journey to visit them. It was incredibly refreshing to observe this lightness within them. Even if they did have many concerns about their lives, their animals, families, and more, rarely did they display it.

To be light and nimble is to have that buoyancy the nomad has within them. Movement is the most important aspect here, and not just the physical movement, but the movement of the mind to make solid decisions under often challenging and potentially life-threatening situations.

The "Congested" Mind = Blockages

A Massai I had the good fortune to meet, Simon Soitanae, told me he believes people in the west—or urban dwellers in "civilized countries"—are too "congested" in their minds. I found this word "congested" interesting as it seems to be the antithesis of light and nimble. Collins Dictionary (2018) states the meaning to be,

> If there is congestion in a place, the place is <u>extremely crowded</u> and blocked with traffic or people, and/or congestion in a part of the body is a <u>medical</u> condition in which the part becomes blocked.

The word that jumps out here is "blocked." I would agree there is a tendency to be blocked at all levels of the food chain of a corporation as well as individually. There is sometimes a blockage when information doesn't cascade down to all vertical and horizontal levels and systems.

❝ If there are too many things, your mind will destruct.

As a leader, I am sure you are blocked from time to time when making decisions, seeing the next pasture, or making personal decisions, whether this is an emotional, mental, or physical blockage. It is apparent, considering the amount of therapy and coaching in our societies of today, this is quite common.

What are the blockages limiting you from being light, nimble, and fast thinking? Are the blockages keeping you from Following the Rain?

Simon had more great insights I would like to share with you:

> People should not get congested on too many things; you should focus on one thing at a time, then you can retain better. If there are too many things, your mind will destruct. It is better to think broadly and focus in on one way forwards. The environment helps us to expand, and you don't have

to use what you don't have. You have to think on what you have and offer not to what you don't have; think to your circumference. Those who think narrowly, they will never go ahead for long; they won't be able to do as much as they don't think outside of the box. Think broader.

> **Think vastly; act narrowly**

These two quotes reflect Simon's thoughts: "Think vastly; act narrowly" and "*yat s yat urd yat f yat*," meaning to put your problems in a queue, not as a pile, and deal with them one by one. Doesn't this sound familiar? In western culture, we say "one step at a time."

The Fear Factor Blocks following the Rain

There are many different factors that may cause people or institutions to become blocked. One reason is fear, and often this is the fear of the unknown. Fear can be debilitating and, in its extreme forms, can paralyze the mind and physical movement. One way to get past fear is to expand your mindset and thoughts.

As Simon says, take one step at a time; break down a large, complex challenge into bite-size, manageable pieces. Break it into chunks, stand back, and move the problem out of you by physically putting the block or problem in front of you (on a piece of paper, a white board, etc.). Then walk around the problem, see it from different angles, and stay outside of it by observing.

The congestion is mostly about piling too many "things" on top of each other in our minds. You cannot see the forest for the trees. This creates blockages or congestion and stops the movement. As the Moroccans say, "you cannot put the whole camel in the pot at the same time, only one piece at a time."

1. How can you be more light, nimble, and fast in your thinking?
2. What are some blockages that might be holding you back?
3. How can you think more vastly?

Follow the Rain's Relationship to Organisations

How does Follow the Rain translate to an organisation or leadership?

There are different evolutionary periods in the growth and trajectory of a company, and most start by Following the Rain: this is the impetus/trigger for something new, the new pasture to graze upon, or the need in the market that hasn't been filled. Then somewhere along the evolutionary journey of the company, something will happen that might congest the thinking. Many factors can cause this: competition, inability to move fast enough into a new market, ego-based leadership, greed, lack of spending on innovation, or simply not keeping the Eyes of the Hawk on the rapidly changing environment (i.e., losing the vision).

There are many examples of corporations that stopped Following the Rain: Nokia, Kodak, Toys 'R Us, Border, and Blockbuster to name a few. Let's take a closer look at what happened with Nokia and how their mindset became congested. Watch for the evolution and the change in mindsets.

Case Study: Nokia—from Nomad to Builder to Settler to Dinosaur?

"Nokia started with a beautiful vision, and then the vision went," Mads Winblad tells me. Mads worked for Nokia from 1990 to 2010 as first the Managing Director for Denmark and then in multiple managerial and leadership roles till he left the company. He agreed to share Nokia's story— how it went from being an innovative, top-notch tech company to becoming so congested that it stopped Following the Rain and ultimately went the way of the dinosaur.

Nokia started with a beautiful vision, and then the vision went 🔸🔸

The Departure plus Nokia's Nomadic Mindset Beginning

In 1990, a new CEO, Jorma Ollila, came to Nokia, and this is when the mobile technology all began for Nokia. Nokia, before this time, was into selling rubber boots, televisions, toilet paper, tables, and forest industry and other products. I was asked to come on board as Managing Director in Denmark. Over the years I was there, I had many positions, which changed considerably. I was invited, at the end of 1990, to a global sales meeting, and the new CEO, who I didn't know of, talked about [how] 'we need to change this organisation as we were not competitive enough.' I thought to myself laughingly, 'what the f . . . is going on? What am I in for now?' He disrupted the organisation, [and] we moved focus from stuff we shouldn't work on to a shared direction, which was mobile phones.

But what he was actually saying was that all the people who had been part of Nokia before didn't really have the competence to move into a new digital area. It would [now] be mobile phones, it would be infrastructure . . . so they should all go home and start to recruit people who maybe came from the computer industry, or whatever, to understand this.

The CEO dismantled the old business and left all of the old products and industries behind, and by 1993, the company was purely digital infrastructure and mobile phones. I had the great opportunity to be part of this innovative revolution—of change—and played a significant role on the journey, which was about changing Nokia.

It is obvious from this early beginning that the new CEO had a visionary and innovative nomadic mindset with his eye on the future looking for new pastures for growth. He was Following the Rain!

New Discovery

As Mads tells me, around 1994/1995, Nokia entered into another discovery phase, heading towards the smart device:

> Already in '94, '95, when I was in Sweden, we started a relationship with Hewlett Packard. HP had at that time, I can't remember what it was for, it was kind of a smart device, but there was no mobile phone integration or whatever, so we started a little bit of that kind of thinking and then back home in the facilities and so on. Nokia obviously bought a company called Cyan at that time, and Cyan had an operative system. They only wanted to take that operative system and build it into a mobile phone. We did that, and then that was how Symbian was founded. Symbian was then later put [in] Nokia's smartphones.
>
> This is when the whole smartphone, or multimedia, as they called it, came into being.
>
> During a two-day conference in Salzburg, Austria, Nokia invited opera-tors and global core partners, [and] 'the purpose was to drive the industry towards this digital consumer direction in the mobile industry.'
>
> Following this, Nokia really kicked into the 'multimedia computer' as they called it at that time. We didn't know the 'smartphone' name at that time, so Nokia actually introduced the smartphone, the multimedia computer, into the industry . . . back in 1996. In 1996 when we introduced Communicator 9000, that was a device where [when] you opened [it] you had a keyboard, and when you locked it together, you could use it as phone.

Mads shared with me an inspiring and curious meeting that his boss, Anssi Vanjoki, led. It is a perfect example of the curiosity, innovation, and nomadic intelligence that goes into risking new pastures by Following the Rain.

> So the story was, Anssi had a slide [on a PowerPoint presentation] with a device with different kinds of logos. It stays like that on the slide, and it was

the only slide, and the device was called Aani. Apparently, there was a guy in Finland, and he is a businessman, and he just got a phone call from a guy in the States, from New York, saying 'You know, we have a very important meeting; you have to come," so he took his device, and then on this slide there was the logo for Finnair, a logo for a hotel chain, a logo for a Finnish insurance company. He just pressed the logo for the airline, and he organized his flight to New York, [and] at the same time, he [pressed] the hotel [logo], and he organized and booked the hotel, he got the receipt, and

You know, we have a very important meeting; you have to come 🔸🔸

so on. Once he arrived in New York, he had more spare time, so he wanted to walk in the city, and then while he's walking, his Aani device started to vibrate, and the logo of the Finnish insurance company came up and was blinking, and then he pressed the logo and [in] comes a text saying, 'Now you are moving into a restricted area, if you go further on, do you want to increase your insurance?'

Let me stop here for a moment and say this story in many ways seems like ancient history compared to what mobile devices are capable of performing today. However, in those days, Nokia was nomadic and highly innovative, grazing in new pastures.

Before this, Nokia already had in '95 introduced the first camera phone, and [at] the end of the 90's, we started to negotiate a contract with Zeiss for the Carl Zeiss lenses, when we started to bring cameras into the mobile devices.

When you are looking [back] at it today, at least two inventions had been driving Nokia phones, and [those were] bringing cameras to the mobile device . . . and bringing smartphones to the market.

From 1993, they would have global strategy sessions and workshops every year to work on vision and strategies for the future. This was then presented to the executive board, and they would choose what we would concentrate on or not. It was a robust and creative time and full of optimism and excitement for these new products and how we were growing globally.

To put what Mads said another way, these were the nomadic and builder mindsets in full swing, producing and innovating with a strong vision.

I was so lucky to be part of that since '93 and the whole way up. [From] 1999 to 2001, we started to say, 'we need to do something to enable our multimedia devices, our smartphones, to have more power, be able to have longer battery time. To do this, we need to disrupt ourselves and slow down the development of the mobile phone with the operative system, which was in the mobile phone, because that's a dumb system. We need to focus on the multimedia computer, the intelligent software systems, we have to change.' This was being felt within the organisation.

Builder/Settler Mindset Settles in

At this juncture, in 2000/2001, things changed, which led, ultimately, to the demise of Nokia and the massive market share they had in the mobile industry. Nokia had now fully entered into a builder mindset, moving years later to a settler mindset.

> **" The rain, as the nomads would say, is life blood.**

What began to happen was the necessary decisions were not made to drive resources away from mobile phones and put more resources into new operating systems for the multimedia devices. Everything was lined up for this as Nokia had a working relationship with Intel, and they were eager to partner in the development of a new operating systems and replace the original Symbian system. This decision to shift and change pastures was, unfortunately, not taken by leadership.

Or, as Mad says,

> It seemed that when the company was not running that good, a disruptive decision was taken to change, and when the company was going well and there was a definite need on the horizon to change and be disruptive, decisions were not [made] to do so.

In many large companies, especially legacy companies that don't shift, something stops them in their incredible vision and direction. This has been documented over and over with different corporate case studies. The rain, as the nomads would say, is life blood. If you don't have rain, you will not thrive or survive. This is when the warrior and wisdom of the elders steps in. This is the place of the leader of the company.

Mads believes the leadership got "greedy and complacent like many others were."

> Around 2000, we started to settle in. And we were too fat and happy. Big bonus plans, Starbucks, all that stuff, it was just too much of the good stuff, and then what happened was, it started to go down[hill].

I have very good relations with one of the guys who was the R&D Manager, and I talked with him and said, 'What could we have done differently now, when we didn't [make] this decision at the beginning of the 2000s?" He was actually on the task force in 2004 to try to do it again and try to save part of Symbian and turn it into something different. He said, 'there were so many restrictions set that were working against it. It was important that we still had the same vision—forwards-looking [and] inspiring—but it was not enough to convince the decision maker. He didn't care anymore. That was in 2004.

Totally Missing the Rain

After talking some more with Mads about the three mindsets, he enthusiastically agreed that Nokia originally had a nomadic mindset:

Nokia was a nomadic company through the 90s and the beginning of the 2000s, then they [headed to] the building phase and then settled in, and finally they were just freezing in the end. The dinosaur was on the horizon.

Mads made this observation with some sadness in his voice—he loved this company and the superior knowledge it once had.

When it really started to go bad, we got the information—I think it was 2005 or something like that—that Apple was coming out with the iPhone, and we who were fighting for this change, we said *this is only a little niche, nothing to be worried about* 'Yeah, we know. This is shit; we need to do something.' Some of the other people, and actually the next CEO, mentioned in the press that 'this is only a little niche, nothing to be worried about.'

What happened there was that we realised that Apple was coming with this, and they are coming from the computer side. We [were coming] from the mobile phone side and trying to move into this computer [side], and we tried to grab in and we couldn't do it. They knew everything about how software should be built from the bottom, what you do for a next version of software update. We were fighting because our basic was not right, and our leadership didn't dare to change the basic in 2000. So, we noticed that they were coming, and if we don't do something with this, they will just take the whole market, and that was what happened.

After the change in leadership in 2006, and the realization [the] iPhone was coming in, Nokia was sunk. Rumours began to swirl around what was going to happen with Nokia and the shareholders, and Wall Street began to get worried. Fast forwards with very little change in direction and declining sales and market share, by 2010 another leader was brought in from Microsoft, which led to the sale to Microsoft —who wanted in the mobile technology industry—of Nokia's mobile phone area. Nokia kept its infrastructure portion, but by 2013, Microsoft got rid of Nokia.

Dinosaur or Comeback? Lessons Learned

Will Nokia make a comeback? Will the phoenix rise from the ashes? Who knows? What is important to learn is the leadership lesson: the keeping of the visionary, nomadic mindset is vital to an institution's success. Have a strong builder mindset, settle for a while, but never settle for too long.

Mads really loved Nokia and stayed there until the sale to Microsoft. He went through the whole process and was involved heavily in the innovative phase and sales.

> The mindset we had in this organisation was that the future is so cool—no matter what we were moving from stone to stone—where we saw some opportunities, and some worked and some didn't work, and then, you know, the whole thing just exploded, and I think that was the mindset.

Nokia was a brand that rocked the world of mobile telephony. They were the most popular phone—and were more popular than their competitors Ericsson and Motorola—in the early stages. They owned the title of market leader in the mobile telephone industry. As Mads observed, "The vision was right . . . it was how it was executed that went wrong."

The Mindsets in Play

Speaking about the nomadic mindset, Mads says,

> I think the mindset of a nomadic company is more about curiosity [about] what can we do rather than when you come into settled organisations, [it's] about numbers, [it's] about cost cutting and all these kinds of things more than about focusing on what is the kind of thinking.

Nokia's leadership had a dominance of nomadic mindset for the first 10 years in direction, energy, output, innovation, and vision. They also had a subdominance of builder and settler mindset. The driver that rallied the other mindsets was the nomadic mindset.

As a leader or CEO, are you willing to keep making nomadic mindset decisions? Or are you congested and settling?

If you want to navigate a company with a long-term vision, you need to have a nomadic mindset; otherwise, you will not be able to do it because you will believe that it just won't work like that. So that's one thing, and if you settle, I don't think settled companies actually work that much with a vision. If they have a vision, it's probably more of a statement that is an active measurable vision of what they are doing.

– Mads Winblad

Why Follow the Rain?

Follow the Rain is about finding new pastures to graze upon and grow. Nomads do not want to overstay one pasture or grassland by over-harvesting or raping the environment. They do not like to ruin the land for future nomads or generations on their return to the area.

In corporate lingo, Follow the Rain means looking with the Eyes of a Hawk for innovations for the future, finding new markets, new directions within the company, purchasing companies to enhance organisational holdings, ways to engage employees, developing entrepreneurial mindsets, and more. It also means timing and strategy are vital. Nokia had all the right timing going for it. It was way ahead of the curve and its competitors like the lead runner in a 1,500 m race who loses focus on the runners behind who are keenly keeping an eye on the market leader and just waiting for the right moment to overtake first place. Then the moment appears, and the leader loses steam and slides back in the pack. Your moment in the rain has passed.

○

When I left Romain Simenel, the French anthropologist, in the beautiful mosque, I felt I had truly Followed the Rain by meeting with him to discover more about the nomadic mindset and corporations.

○

Your objective, should you choose to accept it, is to sharpen your innate intuition and observe—with more vigour—where and when the next rainfall comes. It is what brings growth. Keep a keen eye on the environment (trends), and be careful to let go or move on at the right time. By expanding and migrating to Follow the Rain, you can then Seek the Foie Gras.

○ ○ ○

LEADERSHIP RETHINK

Essential nomadic leadership qualities to embody:

Follow the rain	Risk	Fast
Open	Predators	Hope
Mindset	Expansive	Drive
Observe	Light	Vision
Intuition	Nimble	Explore

FINAL QUESTIONS

1. What does Follow the Rain mean to you? What does your innate intuition say?

2. What is the mindset of your organisation at this time in your evolutionary process? What mindset do you need more of?

3. How valuable is it for you to look at your corporation from the three mindset typologies' perspective?

Seek the Foie Gras

Mission: to turn negative situations into opportunities

◖

"Everything is an opportunity"

– SAID ZAKI, A BERBER,
WORKING FOR CLUB MED GLOBALLY

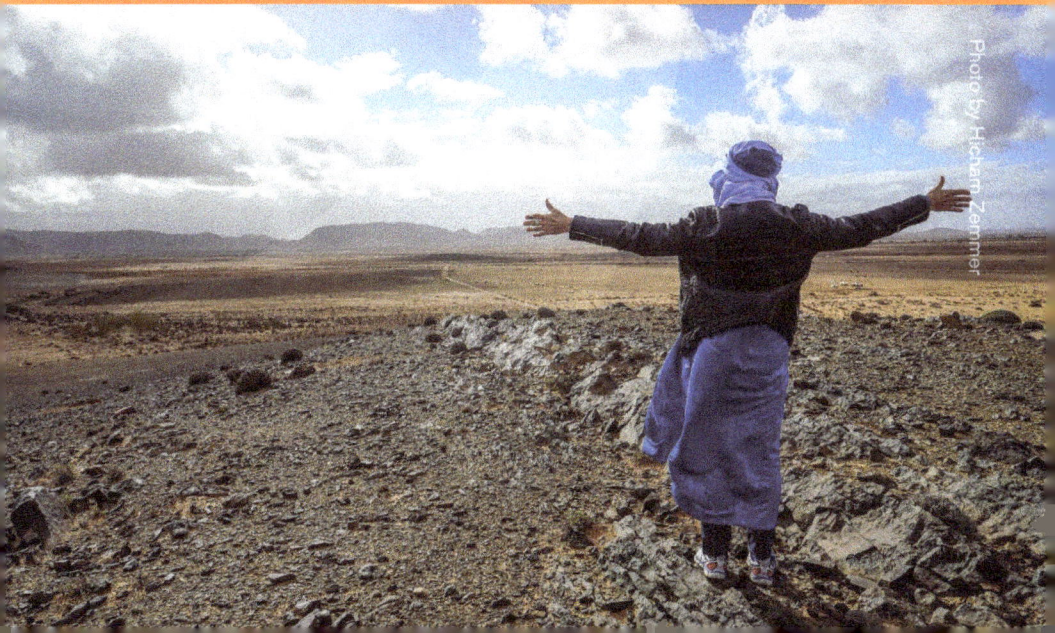

SEPTEMBER 17, 2017, CLUB MED CHERATING BEACH, MALAYSIA

Club Med Cherating Beach, Malaysia, is a dream location to facilitate a Train the Trainer course. Said Zaki, a Berber from Southern Morocco, is a member of my group. After our training, I ask him if we can have a deeper conversation about life as a Berber. One of the first things he says is that Berbers "see everything as an opportunity." What a positive and optimistic outlook! It makes me more curious. He then goes on to share a story about locust swarms and how Berbers refer to this as Foie Gras. Now I am very curious.

> *see everything as an opportunity*

You may have heard of the French food delicacy, Foie Gras: the liver of a duck or goose that has been specifically fattened to produce a rich, succulent, and buttery tasting liver. To get this taste, the ducks and geese are force-fed corn with a feeding tube. Not particularly pleasant for the animals, and today it is often grossly looked down upon in the animal husbandry world.

"We use the image of Foie Gras to explain the story of the locust swarms that come from [the] Senegal River and travel northwards through Mali, Burkino Faso, towards Morocco," shares Said.

Said continues to explain the migration of the locusts:

> The locusts start by eating the greenery around the Senegal River, and as the wind carries this dark cloud of locusts northwards, the skies darken. They will settle for a moment, eating all the greenery, and then move on to more green pastures, growing fatter and fatter. They become filled with all kinds of nutrients and vitamins as they feast on plants, bushes, [and] trees, making the journey north. They are in many ways force-feeding themselves. By the time they get to the southern Sahara in Morocco, they are ready to explode, just like the ducks and geese.

I remember a previous conversation with Romain Simenel, the French anthropologist, who shared a similar experience and story of the Foie Gras:

> When I was in Sidi Ifni in southern Morocco, a swarm of red locusts filled the sky, and all the rich, green argan trees in the area. Everything in the sky and on the trees changed to red, like a fire blazing everywhere. The sound was overwhelming and loud . . . like the earth has been shaved; it is horrible. Wow. The red colour are the females who are pregnant. They land for a few minutes, eating, then off they go again. But you know what the nomads say? 'For us, it is luck.' They say, 'This is meat.'

The nomads savour this moment with anticipation and turn it into a fiesta as they take advantage of harvesting the locusts. The Berbers see the swarm of locusts coming, and they capture the opportunity for abundance. In the night, everyone—boys, girls, mothers, fathers—will take long white tissues and wind them around trees and bushes, like nets and a backdrop (so to speak). Then, they set light to the bushes.

With the flames lighting up the night sky, this light reflects off the white tissue, attracting the locusts to fly into the tissue. Then they rapidly close the tissue and capture the locusts. The nomads then take the harvest of locusts back to

a sign of a good year is a swarm of locusts 〞

their homes and have a feast: the Foie Gras of the Sahara. They will either boil them, or sizzling sounds can be heard from the grilling of the Saharan delicacy. Thus, the nutrients of the Sahara fills their bodies.

Aissa Derhem, the Berber mathematician, also a friend of Romain, says "a sign of a good year is a swarm of locusts."

The Foie Gras Opportunity: A Mindset

The locust feast comes at a cost—what some would consider devastation. All that rich produce, vegetation, and crops . . . gone.

It's most likely those with a settler and builder mindset would be devastated by this destruction. And they certainly have a point—most people would see the negative in this destruction. But not the Berber, not the nomad. Even though they understand the horror of the devastation, they see this as an opportunity to survive and eat rich food.

As Romain observed, "They have this strength to always transform a fatality into an opportunity." This a nomadic mindset quality.

Opportunity to Survive

This locust story is also a reflection about survival. Living in the desert or on the grasslands of the Maasai Mara in Kenya or the steppes in Mongolia is about the opportunity to survive—and thrive if you can. Nature is real, the animals' lives are real, and human nature is real.

How do you survive? How can you thrive? You need to look at all things as an opportunity to survive by finding the possibilities in every challenging situation that might appear in front of you.

Further to the connection between opportunity and survival, I sat down to talk with Ashutosh Srivastava, Chairman and CEO, AMEA and Russia/CIS of Mindshare, a global marketing communications agency. He, too, spoke about seeking out opportunities, eliminating borders, and looking for that Foie Gras customers will consume before moving onto the next Foie Gras.

He says, "In this business, if you are not nomadic, you won't survive." And when it comes to opportunities, especially in his business, he says,

If you went with stuff you invented last year or the year before, there's [since] been fifty other copycats who will do it for that brand and possibly [at] a third or a quarter of the cost . . . we have massive market share only because we don't follow that approach at all.

❝ In this business, if you are not nomadic, you won't survive

The approach is to constantly keep coming up with the new products and services all the time in response to the changes in the environment and brand marketers' needs. There's so many start-ups, especially in the marketing/ad tech and data sector that are not part of a big, global, monolith type. If anything, they are far more agile as their survival depends on their next meal. Unlike us, the large businesses who have hundreds of clients, they are even more hungry and agile, and so our approach is to embrace [them] and bring them in.

When a brief from a client comes, we have people who then look out constantly in the market and keep in touch with those new emerging companies to see how we can co-op them into the solution. Sometimes we take a small stake, not such a big stake that [it] will stop them. This gives us a small strategic stake, which is in our interest as it gives the partners some cash, access to the big brand marketers we work with, and a chance to partner with our teams on these clients.

You need to see the opportunities and agile partnerships plus the risks that exist internally and externally to your corporation. What is your next Foie Gras?

1. What is the swarm of locusts that creates a successful year in your company and your leadership?
2. What are the potential fatalities or negative points you have turned into opportunities of late?
3. In what ways can you encourage a working environment to look at everything as a Foie Gras moment?

Opportunity = The Intelligence of a Nomad

Let's step back for a moment and explain how a few people define the intelligence of a nomad.

> *You need a nomadic mind to connect the dots.*
>
> – Aissa Derhem

> *Nomads are responsible—they already know what their strategy is. They are very logical; they are people who always look for a better chance.*
>
> – Batgerel Bat, Head of the National Branding Council of Mongolia

> *Tribe is a philosophy. It means that it's a kind of a way of thinking [and] a way of seeing life, a way of . . . living in the nomadic world, mindset.*
>
> – Romain Simenel

Nomads are led by nature, and nature's intelligence tells them when to move on ”

The intelligence of the nomad is, in many ways, the mindset needed in corporations today. This is intricately linked to transforming potential negative situations into opportunities and being directly interconnected with nature. In this case, "nature" is your organisational environment and its interconnection with the external environment. When nature delivers opportunities, you must be ready at any given moment to embrace or reject them.

This intelligence allows nomads to Never Settle . . . for Too Long before seeing another potential opportunity. Every move is strategic because it will directly impact the whole tribe, clan, community, family, or nature itself. Nomads are led by nature, and nature's intelligence tells them when to move on.

What metaphoric animals or parts of nature tell you to move on? Is it Wall Street, competitors, new markets, mergers, ideas/creativity/innovation, a little intuitive voice inside of you . . .?

Said Zaki says,

> Berbers and nomads do settle and they modulate their lives with the sand . . . the sand is moving everyday . . . it means living in peace with self and nature . . . it means watching and know when to move on . . . they see this in a clear way. The nomads are in tune with nature . . . they understand what their needs are . . . for me, we should not take something from here and put it there; it doesn't make sense. We need to adapt to the environment.

How do you modulate with the shifting sands of your business?

Seeing Opportunities: Getting to the Starting Line

Seeing the seeds of opportunity, adapting to a new environment, and then doing something about it can be a challenge. On that note, I had a wonderful opportunity to sit down with Grant "Axe" Rawlinson, a New Zealander, an adventurer who now works with companies as a coach and trainer. He related his thoughts around "freedom, adapting to no borders, and opportunities" that he sees in life and also what is needed in the corporate environment. The type of adventuring that Grant does is tough—mentally physically and spiritually. He powers a sailboat with just sails or oars (i.e., no motors) on which he set off on an adventure from Singapore to New Zealand with just one other person. Here is a nomad that sees opportunities and pushes personal mindsets. He shares,

> It is freedom from a life that human beings have created without us even knowing it. Life is incredibly complicated, and you don't realise how complicated it is to live, and without doing anything, just surviving until you have to leave. When I left to go away for a long time, I had to shut down phones, make sure the mortgage would be paid, pay the bills—and set up systems to pay—make sure the family was safe and cared for. It made me realise how complex life has become just to live these days. To stay and live in a developed country these days with the insurances, food, car parking, coupons and permits, servicing, jobs, and relationships . . . wow.
>
> *It made me realise how complex life has become just to live these days* 〞
>
> I always tell people the hard part is getting to the start line—it is not actually being out there— it's actually getting away from the massive system we have created, and when you get out on the expedition, there is freedom. The only thing you think about on an expedition is what you eat, keeping moving, sleeping, going to the toilet. Life becomes extremely simple; it is almost as if how life should be to me.

1. How could you better encourage or influence others to get to that starting line?
2. What does the intelligence of a nomad mean to you as a leader?
3. In what ways can you strategize differently with the intelligence of a nomad in mind?

Borderless: Opportunistic Agriculture

I learned about how "opportunistic agriculture" relates to Foie Gras from the French anthropologist, Romain Simenel:

> It's a spontaneous agriculture. It's kind of an opportunistic cereal culture . . . a nomad always has some wheat seeds that he carries with him. Old wheat, not Monsanto seeds.
>
> Not every year it rains in the desert, perhaps one in every four years with some huge drops. This is when the nomad will plant his seeds. They plant them on the Grara (area/plot/space). The nomad is not like other farmers or agriculturists; he will not watch over his crop. He will leave it for maybe three or four months and then return to see if how the wheat is doing before leaving again.

Romain once asked a nomad,

> 'What if someone comes before you and takes your crop?' The nomad replied, 'No problem, because at first, maybe the nomad should know I normally use this Grara, but if not and he takes the crop of wheat, I will go to another Grara and take that crop.'

Therefore, Romain, with his thick French accent says, "This is the opportunistic way: they plant and go. There is no one saying this is my land, and you can't be here."

Both Foie Gras and the planting of wheat seeds are different aspects of the underlying theme of seeing positive opportunities. They speak against the protectionist philosophy of lack and instead promote abundance for everyone. Opportunities are everywhere and come in different forms. One way to be open to seeing opportunities is to remove the borders in your mind that might be limiting your mindset. Being borderless or having a borderless mindset is prevalent today in the technological internet of things, and this integrates with the interconnectivity of things.

In the Berber world, Romain says this is called,

Trab n Mulana
Mulana = another word for God
Trab = land, or more specifically, 'the land of God'

The nomads say, "nobody can put up their hands and say, 'This is my land!'" They say, "No, all Earth for them is the land of Mulana."

This is an extreme and outrageous thought in today's political and economic environments, with respect to industrial copyright, trademarks, countries, immigration, possession of products, territories to sell, and more. As Romain informed me that "Nomads (from southern Morocco) don't understand when they go north and they see fences—that is outrageous for them."

How did we get from all the land belongs to everyone (or God, for some) to this mine/ours mindset? What if you thought about this from a different perspective? What if instead of ownership, ego, and possession, you turned it into a letting-go, sharing, win-win solution, and enough-to-go-around way of thinking? Is this a terribly naïve thought? Perhaps, yet I suggest a human way forwards.

> *Nomads (from southern Morocco) don't understand when they go north and they see fences— that is outrageous for them* **""**

There are some corporations leaning in this direction who are staying agile and borderless. How are they doing this? Some create smaller teams (or departments or units) that allow more interaction and autonomy of decision making. This removes the borders of hierarchy. It also generally guarantees faster decisions. Some institutions have less bureaucracy by using more technological solutions, which innately have no borders (or fewer of them). A similar great idea is to install smaller incubation hubs within more units or departments so information can flow more directly and faster because of fewer borders.

Are you making good use of opportunistic agriculture?

Tearing Down Borders: Transformation

Nomads believe that going to the desert is therapy. As Romain says,

> It's good for your eyes; it's good for your brain; it's good your heart; it's good for your soul . . . it is a purge, so everything that comes from the desert is gold. For nomads it is transforming. Settlers would say, 'this is hell,' but for nomads, Hell is a paradise!

Just like the locusts or someone taking your harvest of wheat, from devastation comes opportunity. This thinking process is in itself a transformation. This transformational way of thinking can apply to companies. Ashutosh Srivastava, Mindshare CEO, shared his thoughts about breaking down corporate borders as the way of the future—and now is the future.

Every business today is transforming, and why are they transforming? It is because they're unable to keep pace organically with the disruptive changes, to be in sync with the marketplace; therefore, there's the need to do something far more radical to actually aid the transformation. Many people are getting left behind and struggling to cope with the changes. They want to take a leap forwards to transform, then it's another challenge on how to keep up that pace in the future, and this is true for every business.

There are enough disruptions out there; you have booksellers and TV stations, brick and mortar businesses now competing with online retailers like Amazon and Netflix. Uber is disrupting traditional taxi companies. All the so-called legacy companies are trying to transform themselves. That is the journey everyone wants to take, and there is short- to medium-term pain within those companies.

But, say, if you don't respect the boundaries, and you are in a business that does, if you are afraid of making mistakes and getting smacked in the face every now and then, [that] means you're not even taking any risk; therefore, you're afraid to experiment outside the boundaries of your business, [and] it means you will never get anywhere . . .

This sense of transforming a fatality into an opportunity is what Fois Gras is about. It is a quality of the nomadic mindset. Nomads simply don't think about it much; rather, it is the way of life, so they deal with it. The emotional aspect can be there; however, mostly it is a function of existence. Why? Because survival is always on their front doorstep or outside their tents. Even with advancing technology, this preoccupation with survival is always there: land, borders, climate change, their currency in their livestock, and much more. Everyone in modern day life is facing survival, and you are facing this within in your organisation every day.

Freedom of Mindset Allows You to See the Seeds of Opportunities

I found the Mongolians (who are Buddhist), the Maasai (who are mostly Christian), and the Moroccan nomads (who are Muslims) all think about Foie Gras and opportunities similarly. All three nomadic cultures come from different physical environments, languages, faiths, and races yet there is no real difference in their mindsets regarding their concept of land, boundaries, risk, and freedom. This is why they have trouble with this concept of fences, walls, barriers, and borders. Freedom of space is for all, and this brings opportunities.

Strong as the desert
Move as the wind
Soft as the sand
Forever free.
– Kahlid Aoud Al Bdoll

Putting up boundaries or borders in the mind of what people can (or cannot) do, what they can (or cannot) think, what they can (or cannot) say, or what they can (or cannot) create/innovate within your corporation, and even yourself, limits your growth, success, and ultimate performance on the global stage. Look at the different borders and boundaries you and your company have created and consider how you can break them down by allowing more freedom of the mind and physical movement, which will lead to stellar performances. Risk stepping over the border—or better yet, erasing the border!

Where to Start?

1. Set your default nomadic mindset to ask "What or where is the Foie Gras in . . .? Then ask, "What is the potential return on investment?"
2. Ask "what or how would a nomad think or do or say?"
3. Start from the top: you, your board of directors, your shareholders, your executive team.
4. Look internally at your processes and systems: how rigid or flexible are they?
5. Look at the emotional intelligence and what borders exist that can create inflexibility, disengagement, and lack of motivation leading to less agility and speed of performance.
6. Look at your teams and the mindsets that make up the teams. Do you have the right proportion of nomadic, builder, or settler mindset for the teams and projects?
7. Once you have done that, look externally at how you can reduce borders and increase speed.

My adventurer friend, Grant, demonstrates ripping down the borders with this example of how he chooses people to accompany him on his travels:

For my own expedition, what was the type of mindset that I wanted in that boat with me? An older, reliable man who was completely resistant to change, or an Olympic rowing celebrity who was very fickle and unreli-able, OR a young chap who had no experience whatsoever and had a great attitude and [was] seeking an opportunity. For me, it was the character I was concerned about. Is mindset massively important? Yes, it is! In terms of business frameworks, you need different mindsets at different times. I chose the young chap.

When you are searching for the next Foie Gras or opportunistic agriculture, remember to be ready to move and leap to opportunities, turning negative situations into opportunities, while freeing and opening up the borders of your mind. Take a risk. Keep your nomadic mindset alive.

As Ashutosh says, "Each day you need to start afresh because you might have done a great job yesterday, but today you might be outdated.

○

The Foie Gras is such a colourful, visual story shared by Said, Romain, and Aissa about seeking opportunities. Even Ashutosh and Grant had a version of Foie Gras in their different roles and experiences. To seek, reveal, unleash, and seize the opportunity, you need to tear down the borders—be fearless—so you can see the opportunities firsthand. Revolt against the initial negative gut response that most likely happens. To see seeds of opportunity, it takes courage, the desire to risk and explore, and the desire to be free of borders in the mind. Another nomadic mindset wake-up call! There is opportunity in everything.

To seize the opportunity, you also need to Recognize Change as the Nature of Things. Get ready.

○ ○ ○

LEADERSHIP RETHINK

Essential nomadic leadership qualities to embody:

Opportunity	Expansion	Strategy
Fresh	Freedom	Risk
Positive	Borderless	Courage
Right attitude	Agile	Explore
Open	Adapt	Reveal
Curious	Agriculture	Unleash

FINAL QUESTIONS

1. How can you create a more opportunistic and spontaneous agriculture/culture in your organisation?

2. As a leader, what borders and boundaries do you need to tear down: physically, mentally, emotionally, and spiritually?

3. What would freedom look like to you?

Accept: Change as the Nature of Things

Mission: to look at change in all systems and processes as normal

○

"Adapting to new changes is part of the nomadic mindset"
– NERGUI SANDAGJAV, CEO,
REACHFINANCE MFI, MONGOLIA

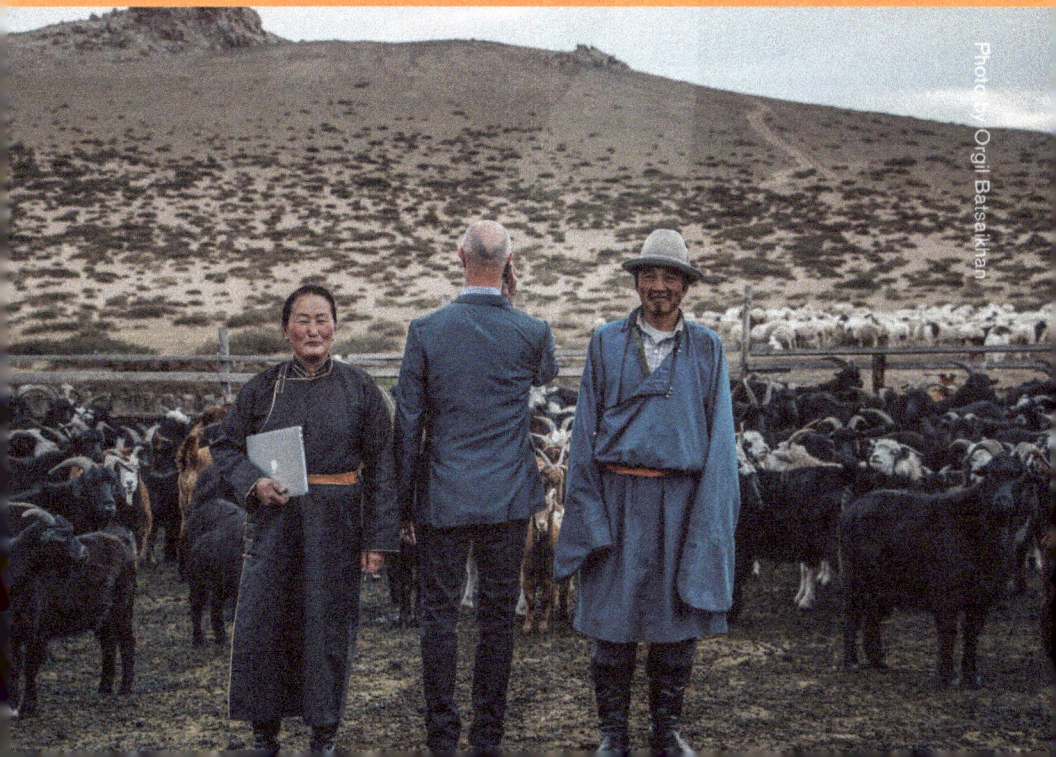

Photo by Orgi Batsaikhan

OCTOBER 1, 2017, ULAN BATOR, MONGOLIA

'm at the Blue Sky Hotel in Ulan Bator, with Fredrik Härén, Esso Khulan Baljinnyam, and Batgerel Bat, and a few other urbanized Mongolians, and I ask them how nomads deal with change in Mongolia. They look at me with a slightly perplexed facial expression. Then Esso says matter of factly, "If something doesn't work out, then we try something else, and we don't spend a lot of time deliberating over it. We just move on."

Just move on . . . after I leave this meeting with my team of Fredrik, Esso, Orgil (my photographer), and Baddy (our driver), we head off in a fancy Mercedes 4×4 to the Mongolian steppes outside the city to stay with Namjildorj Oyun and Ravdan Sanduijav in their yurt. It is getting dark, and the instructions for getting to their yurt are a bit obscure. Esso is on the phone to Namjildori (the wife of our host family), and she says, "At signpost 273, you will see a billboard; turn off there," and that's about it. Baddy continues driving on the highway in the pitch black, and we see signpost 273, but no big billboard, and he turns off the highway onto the fields. There are no lights anywhere, just the stars in the sky.

> **" If something doesn't work out, then we try something else**

Baddy swerves and drives fast across the land, changing freely from one direction to another, searching for the yurt. No one really knows where we are headed, but we remain in good spirits. The whole adventure is humourous. After a while, we decide to return to the highway. Esso gets back on the phone with Namjildori to check for directions again. Baddy decides to go further along the highway and search again until we know we have gone too far. At this point, we don't know what to do, so the only thing to do is laugh, really. Again Esso calls, but this time he calls Raydan, the husband.

Baddy changes direction again, and we head to where we just came from. Finally, we see a billboard and signpost 273. Baddy turns off the highway on a bumpy, rolling kind-of-a-road, again swerving here and there. Esso again speaks to Raydan, who says he will turn the lights of his truck on as a guide for us in the vast black. Back and forth, up and down, swerving here and there, Baddy changes direction back and forth. We are searching for two lights in the distance.

At this point, we have no clue where we are heading, but the Mongolians in the 4×4 are calm and just keep moving on; me, I am getting a bit worried. Finally, after a long journey, Esso spots the lights, and we swerve in another direction to head towards them. We arrive at the yurt, and Raydan greets us, though now there is only time to sleep as it is so late at night.

What has this to do with change? This is an example of Esso's earlier statement, "If something doesn't work out, then we try something else, and we don't spend a lot of time deliberating over it. We just move on."

As Batgerel says, referencing a Mongolian proverb around change, "If a lake is not changing the water, it will go stagnant; change is important." That's a powerful word isn't it: stagnant?

What is stagnant in your leadership or your company that needs to be changed? Do you ever get the feeling you are going around and around on a subject or you keep making the same decisions on projects by using the same old processes you have for years? In many ways, like our adventure into the country, stagnancy invites change—you just need to realise it before it happens.

How do you view change?

Change as Process: The "Seed of a Calling"

As Dr. Sheila Patel, an medical director at the Chopra Centre for Well-Being, said, "change is natural and the only constant in life." She further suggests that, when considering the nomadic mindset, it is comparable to "a seed of a calling and a time for change."

That "seed of a calling" is the way you perceive and interpret change in your life, leadership, and institution. It is in many ways like the Foie Gras. It takes a bold and courageous mindset to see the interconnected ecosystems that surround you and change when it is time to change.

change is natural and the only constant in life 🙶

If so, then change can be thought of as not one singular event but a process made up of a string of interconnected events that creates a continuum. When a corporation goes through a period of change management, it is not one singular event, it is many events making up the change process within the different organisational systems. The events are interconnected in different ways.

Change in Organisations

You are confronted with change in your company on a daily basis, from simple functioning processes to potentially complex, hostile mergers or take-overs. Change runs the size gamut (in micro or macro events) and certainly comes with varying amounts of stress, uncertainty, and insecurity.

"Change is necessary for creation, and it is important to realise that it is all ok; uncertainty is okay," says Sheila. Most of us know of this intellectually; however, it resonates in varying degrees in everyone and in every corporation as it does in nature.

On the subject of change, Cristian Jonsson, Managing Director at Standard Charter Bank in Singapore, notes how frequently he has witnessed the same type of conversation between employees and CEOs:

Employee: 'Are there gonna be any more changes this year?'
CEO: 'Have you endured change every year in the past 5 years?'
Everyone: 'Yes, I have.'
CEO: 'Why do you think it will be any different this year, the next year? Or the year after?'

Sometimes fear increases in people when they hear about change. It can be open-ended fear for some people; for others, it's tentative; and for still others, this is just normal. This is due to the fear of the unknown, and this goes back again to survival.

It is okay to recognize different ways of doing, being, and thinking 🢒🢒

Sheila recognizes this fearful reaction to change and says, "It is okay to recognize different ways of doing, being, and thinking. Yes, change is a constant, and it is simply the nature of things that are now, to come, and that will be."

Nomads do not flinch with change; they experience it fluidly as the natural occurrence of life and nature. It is just part of life, no matter if you lead an organisation, a country, a family, an employee, or an animal, just as in the song from *The Lion King*, "The Circle of Life."

Nomads Can Teach Us about Change

How Does Change Come About?

Since the beginning of time, there has been disruption, and people have adjusted; yet today, many of us have lost that nomad within us and the natural fluid ability to accept, change, and adapt to the disruptions constantly confronting us. From dealing with traffic, to pollution, to hostile mergers, to downsizing, to the death of another person, you name it—disruption is happening everywhere, all the time.

Disruption shakes up your proverbial comfort zone, and that can be good and bad. Not all change is good if it is not handled wisely. For individuals to grow and change, you need to have that primal sense of hunger for something new and fresh (the Foie Gras and Follow the Rain).

Nature teaches you that change is normal. For example, look at the seasons. In many parts of the world, you have four seasons. But when disruption occurs, like pollution, a volcano erupting, earthquakes, burning forests, or using coal for power and heating, this, over time, puts stress on the natural order or the nature of things, as we are seeing today. These events can affect seasons and climate change, which we are experiencing around the globe.

> **Nomads have a 'trust-and-try-it' mindset whereby if it doesn't work, just leave it, move on, and if it works, go for it.**

The early nomads, because they were interconnected with nature, felt and experienced disruptions on multiple levels. Due to their innate intelligence and insight, they knew they had to change or perish.

I met Nergui Sandagjav, CEO of ReachFinance MFI in Mongolia, which supports and offers microfinancing to Mongolian nomads, at Fredrik Härén's book launch in Ulan Bator. She supports this thought of nomads' innate intelligence and their unique qualities. She says, "Nomads have a 'trust-and-try-it' mindset whereby if it doesn't work, just leave it, move on, and if it works, go for it." She also mentions another quality of nomads: "They won't think so long and carefully about something; they will try, change, and adapt very rapidly." Nergui finds this quite opposite to the west, where, as she says, "They will think about all the consequences and problems and think about it too much, too long, and take too much time; we just try it."

Maybe then, we need to listen to the nomadic intelligence—the nomadic mindset within us. The innate resilience of the nomad, which resides in all of us, is what allows them to flow with the nature of things (disruption), to change, accept, and adapt with a sense of fluidity and calmness.

The Change Cycle

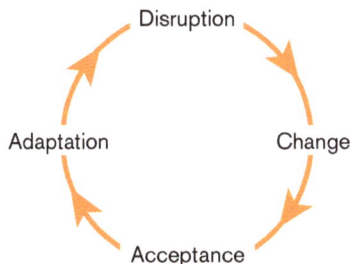

Nomads' Ability To Adapt to Change

One of the great attributes of the Mongols is their ability to rapidly adapt to change. There are a few reasons they are able to adapt so quickly. One is because they are more generalist in their skills and thinking (although today they are becoming more specialized), and another is curiosity. They have less boundaries or borders in their minds, allowing them more freedom.

Nergui says,

> We allow adaptation. In our culture, we like trying new things. I think we are very good at this, and like our culture, it is one of the forces for development. It is something in our mindset, and it is still really existing. We are quick to adapt. This comes from the nomadic mindset.

How do you allow adaptation to happen in you and your leadership?

Mongolians have earned a reputation, even outside their own country, for their ability to adapt easily. Nergui mentioned that South Koreans like to hire Mongolians because,

> They work hard, adapt easily, and their productivity is high. I think this is because they are not afraid of change and take on responsibilities because of their nomadic independent mindset. Even though there is some low level of complaining, they accept, adapt to new things, and change faster than most.

Change: The Fear Quotient

This disruption, change, acceptance, and adaptation cycle all circles back to something else Esso, one of my Mongolian team, said to me when I asked how Mongolians deal with fear. She said,

> We don't do fear. We are not driven on fear. We are driven on trust and how we can keep this nomadic mindset during the changes to urbanization. The balancing of adaption to new things brings the positive of the new things, which is important.

With any disruption or change, fear is generally the natural default system. The fear of the unknown and uncertainty. I found Esso's statement quite insightful and revealing of the Mongolian people and their culture.

I asked Nergui, "Where does the inner drive come from?" She responded with, "the nomadic mindset, I think; yes, that's it."

Mongolians and other nomadic cultures, with their nomadic mindset and outlook on life, have a lot to teach everyone, especially visionary leaders as civilisation moves forwards into the future.

Consider these words from Benson Kipolonka Muntere, a Maasai from Kenya:

> Being a human-being, you must go undergo different stages; you must change because change is a rule of life and is always adaptable. When you were child, you were small, and then you are not. It is a rule of life and is always adaptable.

So true. I invite you to take a few moments to muse upon some of the changes you've experienced in your life. There's likely too many to remember, so pick a few.

1. What was the disruption that triggered the need/want to change?
2. What was the change?
3. How well did you accept and adapt to the change?

What do you think you can do within your company to assist and smooth over the change process and dispel fear, so that others are able to adapt more easily while staying engaged?

How Nomadic Thinking Can Influence Change in Organisations

Cristian Jonsson works for a multinational bank (Standard Charter Bank in Singapore), and you would think banks are the least nomadic organisations because their whole premise is to be settled. I had the opportunity to talk to him at length about his experience, viewpoints, and opinions around disruption, change, acceptance, and adaptation—the change cycle—in the banking industry and its relationship to mindset. He starts off with how nomads equate to change:

> I think change is a must in today's corporate life, whether you work in a bank, whether you work in retail, in a corporation or whatever you do, so unless you embrace change, you get left behind. I do think banks are becoming more nomadic, but they are probably quite settled. In the next five or ten years, they are going to have to change.

Change in many corporations can go sideways at times if you aren't careful. Cristian suggests some possibilities why:

> When you've settled in a place, you get very comfortable where you are, and, at least from what I've experienced, rather than embrace change, you'll always look for negatives of why change is not a good a thing for either you, individually, or for your team.

Or . . .

> When people feel that this change will lead to job insecurity, less reward, no recognition, if what they are doing means nothing, whether it is good or bad, that's when you get disillusionment, lack of energy, and you don't get results.

Or . . .

> Changing pastures to me is not a negative, but it becomes negative if you develop a fear that something's going to happen to you or the team that you are in.

Or . . .

> If I were to sit around and constantly demean the group decision to make a change, or the chief's decision to make a change, then I'm not sure they would want me to be part of that nomad group, which would lead to insecurity. I feel that when I look around, and it is like this in all organisations, in my view, there's always individuals who just don't embrace decisions or changes, and unfortunately, they do get left behind. It doesn't mean that they lose their jobs, it is just that they don't grow.

The qualities mentioned here are those often commonly associated with the settler mindset: comfort, security, and fear. Yet Dr. Sheila Patel believes "insecurity is okay." And, for those who have challenges with coping rapidly with disruption and change, the settler mindset could be a limitation. When an institution has too many employees (at all levels) with this mindset typology, there is potential for it not to move forwards, change, and grow, hence possibly leaving it vulnerable to losing shareholder value, its position in the marketplace, and trust with its employees.

❝ insecurity is okay

What might be an answer to this?

Cristian thinks it is important for leaders to be able to communicate to all people well, and more specifically, to those with a dominant settler mindset in a way that is clear, clean, and supports them while also addressing their multiple fears. Most of those fears or "false expectations appearing real," can be a primal response linked to survival. On the other hand, if you think of change from a nomadic mindset, Cristian suggests,

> Nomads think differently around change. I don't think the whole group just packs their houses up and moves aimlessly without everyone thinking. That would be stupid. I think they all buy into it.

> I feel for nomads it is probably not change because they move as a group, and there's a kinship in the group. There is a positivity around the group and a real systematic, rational approach to why they do things. Everyone is communicated with, people feel secure in the move, they see the positives; there's clearly risks, but they understand the risks."

I don't think the whole group just packs their houses up and moves aimlessly without everyone thinking 🔸🔸

Nomads have to be strategic and focused for the survival of the community, as any leader ought to be. When a nomad moves from one location to another, they must secure the road by identifying the risks to their best abilities, and the same goes for a leader in a corporation or in politics; you need to secure the road ahead, so everyone will buy in and follow. Cristian continues,

> To handle very rapid change, you need to feel you own it, you need to like it, and the way you like change is if you can feel secure in it, right? And you feel somehow protected. At the end of the day, most people that I know have families, they need to pay bills, they want to get rewarded for good work, and they need to understand if I do this then that yields a specific result for them and the team, both on a social and financial level.

You need to communicate sincerely and be responsible for whatever happens (no passing the buck, no blaming). Choose a positive way forwards. Disruption, change, acceptance, and adaption is normal and natural. Bring this to the forefront, and do not shy away from it.

When you want to influence people, be simple in your communication, as Cristian suggests. Go slowly at first and lay out the whole systemic change process. Remember, settlers are the vital glue of your company and can make it run smoothly or not. Therefore, when managing teams, understanding their mindset typology is important.

Cristian believes,

> If you don't manage change within the group, then I think that the group you have can disintegrate, people can leave, and people can get disenfranchised because they don't understand why there's a requirement to embrace change or, in terms of this research piece, to be nomadic.

In organisational teams or tribes or clans, it is important to find out what binds your employees besides the project they might be working on or the overall purpose of the company; it could be friendship, culture, or interests. With this bond, the risks become less as they are all in it together. Yes, there can be dissenting independent voices, which is normal; however, it is the bond of kinship and belief in the direction that will inspire them.

This takes a leader who has a will composed of independent, expansive, and inclusive thinking, feelings, and perspectives and delivers this through, I repeat, communication that is simple and clear, not complex and muddy.

If you view change as a positive thing, rather than something to fear, you open yourself (and your corporation) up to opportunities: the Foie Gras. This is a nomadic mindset.

Cristian explains it like this:

> I think a nomad, from a corporate standpoint, is someone who always looks for the positive reasons to make a change, balancing the risks and rewards, rather than always looking at it from a negative standpoint, and then having the energy to do that.

> You need to communicate clearly down and ensure you have people who are positive around the team, even if you don't always know exactly the end game. You need to encourage, looking for the positives, and then I think that yields positive results.

The cascade of information needs to flow downwards, all the way down, without missing any level of the institution, just like in the tea ceremony. It cannot be vacuous information but real information that will encourage disbelievers and support those on board. It is not just words but actions by the leadership walking their talk with deep respect for everyone else that create positive results. This is a nomadic principle of governance, ensuring support and the positive ways forwards while still understanding the risks.

Being Nimble Helps Secure Change

Imagine you develop and create nimble, fast-moving, interconnected small clans or tribes who are given more autonomy. In addition, you have a small tribe of innovators in each department rather than just one large innovation hub within the company. Allow each small tribe access to the smaller innovation hub, so they can directly interconnect and share information and work together; this allows for more collaboration, faster-moving information, and the ability to adapt more easily.

Considering this idea, Cristian says,

Companies that are very nimble, able to adapt, and who may be viewed as extremely nomadic, can allow for jumping from one place to another and always looking for the next place to go. One of the reasons they are able to do that is that they are either working [in] small units where their chiefs (managers) allow them to jump around, and if they do that, they get rewarded and they can feel secure in that change. They also allow people to be entrepreneurial or intrapreneurial. Unless you are very nimble, unless you are investing in that change or trying to understand that change, then I do think your pasture is going to dry up.

Naturally Moving Forwards

Cristian says that people don't always agree with the change, and he cites his situation:

In the latest change, I didn't necessarily agree with it. I made those points, but once a decision has been made, I think the positive nomads embrace the team, the decision, and get behind it. Once a team has decided to change, if you are part of the team, then you back the team even if you didn't agree with everything that was decided.

Embracing a nomadic mindset can certainly assist you in looking at the change cycle—disruption, change, acceptance, adaptation—in a more powerful way to naturally move forwards. There are obviously many different factors that can go into creating an organisational eco-system that will flourish in these rapidly moving times. One factor that can assist you is understanding the qualities of the nomadic, builder, and settler

It comes down to clear and exact communication **"**

mindsets. Cristian reiterates it very simply, "It comes down to clear and exact communication."

Habib El Bellayni, from the Casbah Museum in Tighmert, Southern Morocco, shared this wise nomadic Arabic proverb with me, which I sense fits this conversation around change:

If you like honey, you must support the bite of the bee.

What do you think this means?

> In the desert,
> nomads follow their life.
> Their animals lead the way.
> They eat;
> they have family;
> they have community;
> they trade;
> they save for the hard days;
> and they Follow the Rain.
> Even though change is slow,
> they adapt rapidly because this is inside them.
> This takes adapting to the environment that is ever changing
> and the circumstances of life that are thrown at you constantly.
> You must accept and adapt to the challenges of life with your eyes fully
>   open.

○

From the craziness of the drive to the steppes the night before and the pitch-black sky full of stars to the next morning, I awake in the yurt; natural change has happened. The day is a new day. I look outside and can't believe my eyes. The expansive nature of the rolling, light brown, grassy steppes in the soft morning light, in places looking like velvet, the animals grazing off in the distance, and the sweet silence in the air, has me disbelieving that just hours before we had travelled over this beautiful land. Change is normal: it is time to migrate to your new day.

○ ○ ○

LEADERSHIP RETHINK

Essential nomadic leadership qualities to embody:

Positivity	Adaptation	Listen
Disruption	Flexibility	Fear
Security	Nimble	Bonds
Healthy	Communication	Support
Clarity	Change	Solidarity

FINAL QUESTIONS

1. How can you communicate the disruption, change, acceptance, adaptation change cycle for better results?

2. What if you were to understand that each mindset typology responds differently to change. How would you communicate then?

3. What are some innovative ways you can lead a change management or reshuffling process?

RETHINK

Develop Respect and Trust

Mission: be consistent in your words, deeds, and actions

C

"When a head starts to get hot, the other head must stay cool"

– ARABIC PROVERB

JANUARY 6, 2018, TIGHMERT, SOUTHERN MOROCCO

Habib El Bellayni from the Tasouavite Tribe, the overseer of the Casbah Museum, is holding court in his tent in Tighmert, southern Morocco. Having visited him a couple times before, I ensure I'm more prepared for our conversation this time. My goal is to ask him some questions specifically around trust.

As I walk into the tent, I see it's filled with jewellery, carpets, teapots, urns, cooking pots, and all sorts of nomadic products for sale. It resembles a museum gift shop. He sits in a corner on the floor on colourful, nomad-designed, carpeted cushions, with his tea kettle heating up and a tray with five tea shot glasses lined up beside him. His other guests and I sit across from him on low, carpeted cushions, relaxed and at ease thanks to his smiling face, robust laughter, and joyful tone. Habib wears a traditional, beautiful blue turban and long, flowing kaftan.

Because he is a master tea maker, he performs the traditional tea ceremony with the three cups of tea, and we eat dates. I ask where I should put the pits, and Habib hands me a dried camel's hoof that doubles as a plate—or even an ashtray. I look at it with curiosity, and Habib laughs with gusto.

Habib doesn't speak English, and because I have enlisted the aid of a translator, the pace of the conversation is much slower, so we languish over the tea while sinking into the pillows and eating dates. Because of the Brahim connection (my translator is trusted here), a layer of formality is removed, which allows respect and trust to build much faster.

We speak about various topics: his family's slave ancestry, the importance of Following the Rain, how they know when the rain will come, the qualities one needs to lead, a story about Habib escaping the intoxicating spray from a hyena on his camel one dark night, and, lastly, how to build trust.

When a head starts to get hot, the other head must stay cool 🍊🍊

He stresses that in the harsh reality of life and the conditions in the desert, respect is vital in building trust if you are to survive the elements.

How many times have you heard people say it takes a long time to build trust and nanoseconds to destroy it? The Arabic proverb, "When a head starts to get hot, the other head must stay cool," gives an indication of how you can manage and build trust. You have two minds: hot and cool. First, you need to consciously be aware, internally and externally, of what your mindset is thinking and of your words, deeds, and actions at all times; this is staying cool.

Getting hot under the collar may not gain respect or build trust. You want to be aware that your mind, heart, and mindset must balance the two sides of the coin equally—the hot and cool—because trust will be the result of gaining respect from your consistent and congruent actions, words, and deeds.

How Do You Build Trust in Organisations?

Surviving the relationships in organisations is as vital as it is for the nomads, and this comes from strong, trusting, and respectful leadership. To be respected and trusted from the bottom up, your respect and trust must cascade all the way downwards to your employees, partners, and customers to ensure the survival of all and a successful corporation. This way you can thrive together.

Habib tells me respect and trust are part of the intelligence of the nomad, and it doesn't matter if you're a businessperson, a holy person, a herder, or a family member; the consistency of respect and trust is part of the intelligence.

> We will share different experiences and knowledge and the tribes will meet up, connect, and discuss situations and what is the best way forwards. They will get together and discuss what are new trends in business, for example, or where the rain is. We are a sharing culture without holding back, and greed doesn't exist in our culture. They say thanks to God, and as long as they have food on the table, they are comfortable, happy, and satisfied.

So, how do you build trust? This is heard throughout all layers of any company. Research says, in general, lack of trust in many corporations can lead to disengagement and lack of motivation, leading to decreased performance levels.

"Trust is so low . . ."

No one trusts the leader . . ."

"You can't trust your team members . . ."

"I don't trust my boss . . ."

"I don't trust this process . . ."

Sound familiar? What nomadic cultures suggest, and what we can all learn from, is that we build trust by first gaining respect.

You need to have the mindset qualities of a respectful warrior in these hard-truth conversations, where you can gain respect and build trust, if you do it in the right manner.

1. What do you need to do to be more transparent in the way that you conduct your conversations, negotiations, and decisions?
2. Reflect upon how you are gaining respect by asking someone who will be truthful to you and not just say what you want to hear.
3. How far down in your organisation does respect and trust penetrate?

The overall question here is, how do you create or build trust in your institution?

Start with Gaining Respect

Habib tells me that "building trust is vital, and to gain respect, you must first respect each other."

This is not the first time I have heard this. In many other conversations with nomads, one of the most prevalent topics was respect. This word came up frequently when speaking about how much they respect their elders, family members, community, specific individuals, and their animals. Respect, with nomadic cultures, starts from the early beginnings of life. It first starts with family and community. This leads to their deep respect for their livestock as that is their currency, ensuring they eat, have a roof over their heads and can do business.

building trust is vital, and to gain respect, you must first respect each other 🟧

I ask them, "How do you build trust?" and they looked at me, as they often did, with a perplexed expression. Any of the nomads I asked this question of, more often than not, would not answer as I sense they thought this to be an odd question. For them, I observed, it is just human nature to respect and trust.

When they did answer, they would say,

> Prove yourself,
> walk your talk, and
> be consistent in your words, actions, and behaviours
> in all your walks of life.
> You cannot act as one person at work,
> then differently with clients,
> or [your] employees,
> or at home,
> or with friends.
> Congruence and consistency are keys to
> building trust
> through gaining respect.

Societies either function and prosper or crumble and wither because of these two qualities: respect and trust. Sadly, in today's world, you see a lot negativism and fear, leading to lack of respect and trust, which then affects motivation, engagement, and performance.

In today's ever-changing, disruptive Industry 4.0 world with the speed of digital transformation, one needs to be careful, take a step back, and ensure respect for individuals, processes, and clients throughout your organisational ecosystem. It is too easy to get so wrapped up in the speed and transformation that the human factor and basic needs are overlooked.

To illustrate this point, I will share a few nomadic stories, which may seem unusual—and perhaps humourous—but I encourage you to view them as nature's metaphors or mirrors for how important gaining respect and building trust can be.

Case Study: The Dromedary Experience

There is another Arabic proverb that says, "Camels are the ships of the desert." This is very true, and in my journey to seek out nomads, I encountered many camels along the way, so it's only fitting they should make their way into this book.

I also encountered the camel's cousin, the dromedary, which you may be less familiar with. What is the difference between a camel and a dromedary? Camels exist in Central Asia, China, and Mongolia. Dromedaries inhabit Africa and the Middle East. A camel is a two-humped ungulate, and a dromedary (drom for short) has one hump. As peculiar as it may sound, metaphorically, the qualities natural to a dromedary, on a higher level, represent many leadership qualities leaders possess today:

- Droms need to build strength (for themselves and their company).
- Droms have a trusted hierarchy.
- Droms need space to roam.
- Droms always remember.

Let me explain further.

Droms Need to Build Strength

It's January 6, 2018, and Brahim Tahero drives Salem (my guide and translator), Hicham (my photographer), and me to the Saturday morning Dromedary Auction Market. We arrive, and I'm amazed to see it's not just a market for buying or selling droms—there are also vendors selling clothes, house products, vegetables, meat, goats, sheep, and other items. All the products are separated into different areas of the market. I find the loud, energetic sound of vendors yelling out their products and enticing customers to their stand enthralling. The women wearing colourful hajibs and kaftans and men wearing darker kaftans all mingle seamlessly together.

As I wander along stopping, looking, and taking photos of the fruits and vegetables, Salem educates me on the different spices and herbs and ways and means of bartering. I breathe in the pleasant incenses and herbs wafting through the air, as well as the sometimes distasteful smell of animals in the distance. The vibrance and speed at which the vendors work with approaching buyers is a sight to behold.

At the drom auction market, Salem answers my questions about the droms. I notice some of the males droms have their legs tied together, and Salem explains it stops them from running off, fighting, or claiming a female. The potential buyers examine the droms' mouths, teeth, and hooves; they run their hand over their heads; they look at their height, length, and width; then they bid in a casual, ambivalent, almost emotionless manner. The droms, I notice, all look docile, with big, sad eyes, yet they possess a laidback, calm, majesty and superiority as they watch over everyone. I catch some of them looking at me. These camels have a lifespan of forty to fifty years, so they could be considered leaders, some more imposing than others.

I catch some of them looking at me 🙶

Drom herders will look for droms longer in body type than height due to the need to transport goods. To build their strength, their owners start training them by taking them a short distance with lighter loads and then keep building their strength and stamina with heavier loads and longer distances. In many ways, this oddly enough mirrors an employee's initial stages within an organisation: the interview and hiring process, the onboarding process, the probationary months, then onwards to moving up the ladder. I also saw parallels here to the long initial search and then the relationship building that corporations undergo when hunting for an executive.

How have you built your strength and stamina? What is the process in your company to help build the strength of your employees? What if you looked at the mindset of each person? How would this strengthen them and your institution?

Droms Have a Trusted Hierarchy

In the drom hierarchy, a chief male drom (azuzal) watches out for the many female droms (saydah) in his harem, so to speak. In the Sahara, when the droms are out grazing, the chief drom is usually found majestically munching away on his food, standing tall and watching to see if everything is safe and sound. Then he will go back to eating or wander to another area of the desert and watch again like a leader or a manager connecting with their clans, tribes, or teams—face to face or virtually.

Droms sort out their hierarchy amongst themselves. The chief drom is normally an older camel, and though he will reproduce with twenty to forty females, he still chooses a mate using his sense of smell. He will fight for leadership of the females and guard them, fighting off intruding droms since he does not like to share his females. The females trust the chief as he has proven himself and gained their respect.

In this comparison, "females" could potentially represent people, projects, or positions. Now, while human leaders do not smell who they hire, they do go through a rigourous talent search process to find the right people for their teams. A comparison can also be made to the way some leaders fight for leadership.

Normally, the older droms are sold for the meat, and they keep the young to grow old; the females are for producing milk and offspring. They keep the strongest of the droms to protect the caravan, which includes a minimum of fifty droms that can go up to 200 km before stopping for water. Half the droms in the caravan are for transport and half are for selling. This is nature's hierarchy in technocolour.

Salem and my other guides informed me that when a caravan sets out to trade with others, it is made up of only men, and the women stay home. Nomads, too, generally have one chief in the group.

In what ways does this metaphor relate to your leadership? Are you respected in your role as leader?

Similarity, on this point of leadership and hierarchy, in the Maasai culture, there is a proverb that says, "A neck will not overtake a head," meaning you can-

> **A neck will not overtake a head**

not overtake the elder as he has wisdom. These nomadic cultures all speak about the hierarchy, whether it be the holy man in Morocco or the elder in Kenya and Mongolia. Respect comes with age. As you age, you gain more respect because you have more wisdom than a younger person. Wisdom is paramount in nomadic cultures and brings respect, which leads to trust if your actions are congruent and consistent.

Therefore, to gain respect and trust as a leader, no matter your age, you also need to have the extra quotient, wisdom, to effectively transcend a thriving organisation. You certainly see this in some corporations and government offices.

What is the difference between a leader and an elder? Lilian Naisola Maloi, a Maasai single mother, said, "Leaders can be anybody, no matter the age; an elder cannot. We have an age for the elder. Elders [also] have a born wisdom, and a leader can learn wisdom." This infers there is a strong element of innateness, spirituality, intuition, or DNA connected with a wise elder or a holy man, yet this is not necessarily the case for a leader because some wisdom can be learned through education.

Wisdom comes from many sources, but should you wish to become a wise leader, consider the following:

- Have a nomadic mindset.
- Possess a spiritual curiosity view of the world inside and outside you.
- Meditate daily.
- Engage your senses.
- Spend time in nature.
- Observe the world around you from a distance.
- Expand the openness of your mind.
- Be nonjudgmental.
- Be insightful.
- Be knowledgeable.
- Be grateful.
- Respect all things in nature.
- Commit to nonviolent communication.

Droms Need Space

Droms get nervous if they don't have space, so they need expansive areas to meander in.

Consider how this relates to having enough space in your incredibly busy and demanding schedule of internal meetings, travel, client interfaces, or even your physical space. The latter can also refer to creating the right environment for the different mindset typologies to work together. Understanding the mindsets can lead to a more effective, motivated, and engaged workplace.

1. What do you do to create enough space to reflect?
2. How can having the right physical space gain respect and build trust?
3. What would being more aware of physical, mental, and emotional space do for engagement and the needs of the different mindsets working together?

Consider the concept that an energetic physical working space or environment is an element that can help gain respect and build trust because people then feel more at ease, which leads to greater engagement. As Linda Locke, Branding Specialist in Singapore, shared with me, "You can apply the mindsets interestingly in the area of real estate. Most companies build one kind of area—I don't get it—you aren't getting the best out of your people."

Relating space to the different mindset typologies, you can generally observe the following:

1. Nomads don't mind wandering around.
2. Builders want their own fixed space, often with a door.
3. Settlers like to have all sorts of things around them to feel comfortable, and they are generally fine in the open area concept.

Not everybody has the same space requirements or views on space, and if they hate their working space, they may be potentially less productive. Just as how droms become agitated when in confined spaces, workers forced to do their job in a space that does not fit their mindset will likely also become unnerved, distracted, and not as efficient as they could be.

Curious as to how droms respond if they are limited by space? Salem told me they'll make white balls in their mouths and spit them out if they are angry. And if they drink rain water from a puddle that has been sitting for days, they will go a bit crazy.

I won't try and make a comparison to a crazy drom, but do be mindful of drinking from stagnant puddles: it may lead to serious disrespect and lack of trust! What this is really saying is that the working space within an institution is an important part of engagement, productivity, and performance.

Of course, you cannot please everyone all the time. It is not about designing spaces or open work stations just to be on the leading edge of design. However, if you understand the mindsets of individuals, you will have great knowledge as to what makes them happy, keeps them engaged, and ensures they perform at their best, and then you can design the space for their needs.

Consider your corporation's space. When you are designing or redesigning your work spaces, do you take into consideration the different mindsets of people? What might the compound effect be for productivity?

Droms Always Remember

Perhaps you have heard the saying "An elephant never forgets." According to Salem, there is a similar saying about droms:

> ❝ You should never frappe (hit) a drom

"You should never *frappe* (hit) a drom. Droms have incredible memories, and they will remember what you did to them, which could potentially erode the trust between owner and drom. If the owner continues to hit and disrespect them, the drom could possibly run away and take the female camels with them."

Because of this, establishing trust and respect with your drom is crucial. As Mohamed Billa, a nomad in the Southern Sahara, says, "Without a drom, you cannot live in the desert; you must respect them."

Another guide I had, Bamal Boujemaa, shared a story with me about a drom herder who hit one of his droms so often that when the owner was not looking, the drom took his females and left the owner for over two years. When the owner finally found them, he made amends with the drom, and they returned. Bamal didn't share with me how the owner made amends, however. While this might sound like an old wives' tale, Bamal assured me it was true.

What has this drom story got to do with respect and trust?

Respect is a value that doesn't belong only to humans. If you have owned an animal before, you know they can teach you a lot about respect and trust. For example, as in the drom story, if you are mean to or abuse your dog, they could become very aggressive or psychologically so nervous around you they might lose control of their sanitary habits.

In this example, respect had to be earned from the owner so the drom would trust him. If the drom was disrespected, it would react accordingly, and trust was lost. This is exactly the same for humans. This may seem simplistic; however, we, as the owners of deep and complex thinking, have the capacity to see that simple actions, behaviours, and words speak volumes to all individuals. Respect and trust are two of the most basic values of human existence.

Imagine you have a leader, or maybe even a peer, who is consistently getting on your case, lying to you, blaming you for your actions, or calling you out in front of other people. How would all this "hitting" affect your respect and trust for that person?

What might happen to your engagement, motivation, or productivity? If you, as the leader, went around and apologized, would this rectify the situation? Do you think you, the leader, would be trusted at first glance, or would it take time?

As the nomads have said, you need to prove yourself and gain respect before you build trust. You must be consistent and not waver back and forth between proving you deserve respect and then acting with disrespect. Congruence and consistency of actions, behaviours, and words need to connect for trust to be gained. Do you need to be more consistent and congruent to get your message across and build an organisation based on respect? When it comes to respect and trust, what do you want your company to be known for?

> *Respect is a value that doesn't belong only to humans* **"**

Engagement Leads to Trust

One of the major challenges within corporations today is engagement. In many ways, you could say engagement is a result of respecting and trusting leaders, managers, and peers.

My friend, Aissa Derhem, in Sidi Ifni, Morocco, told me about his father, Si Hmad, who was an incredibly successful Berber businessman in Morocco, Mali, and Mauritania. Si Hmad was a religious man and lived a humble life, even though he had made a lot of money and was very successful.

Aissa said that one of his father's best qualities was his expansive leadership and belief that the money he made was to be fed back into the business, so he could create places for people to work, grow, and engage. Aissa said his father used to say, "It is better that I build a factory so that it can serve many people rather than showing off with a very big and expensive home."

For Si Hmad, it was about serving the people, so they could grow their skills, talents, and livelihood. He said, "To engage people, [they] need to know that you care about them and that you are working for them to learn and to grow in a true an honest way."

Today, the typical mindset is that employees work for the leaders and the corporation rather than the other way around. What is your opinion on this? Who are you working for: shareholders, Wall Street, your boss—who? When a leader is being of service to the employees, how do you do think this could help engagement, respect, and trust?

> **" It is better that I build a factory so that it can serve many people rather than showing off with a very big and expensive home**

One day, a buyer came to Si Hmad and told him he wanted to buy tea. He stated the price of the tea. The buyer didn't buy at that time, but he came back months later and said he now wanted to buy the tea. He was expecting a higher price to be offered, but Si Hmad gave the buyer the same price he had months earlier. When the buyer questioned this, Si Hmad said, "That was my word, and even though prices have gone up, I told you my price, and I will not change my word." This began a long, collaborative relationship between both parties as trust had been gained through respect. This respect and engagement was honoured on both sides of the relationship.

Trust is only built if all the correct factors exist, and we can see by the wisdom of the nomad that engagement happens by trusting the leader is there for the employee and vice versa. Aissa said that when "you give your word, that is the rule, and if you don't stick to your word, this will get around, and people will not do business with you." This gains respect, and these types of consistent actions and behaviours lead to trust and can further lead to collaboration. Therefore, a possible respect and trust mantra might go something like this:

Respect and Trust Mantra

Consistent,

Congruent,

Worthy,

Actions/Words/Behaviours

and Integrity

gain

Respect

and

Engage

a relationship

that leads to

Trust

Walk Your Talk

So, how do you gain respect and build trust as an individual, institution, or government with your strategic partners, customers, and most of all, your employees? As you reflect upon these metaphors— the drom and the nomads' stories—always remember people with different mindsets respond differently to

Turn the mirror back on yourself

the weight they put on gaining respect and building trust. From a logical point of view, you don't need research to understand these fundamentals qualities of being a human being. It is natural and normal to want this. Turn the mirror back on yourself. Look back at the nomads for this instinct–it lives within you.

Try out the following mantra and see what comes of it:

Prove yourself through your words, deeds, knowledge, and actions.
Be congruent and consistent.
Be honest.
Be courageous and brave.
Experience life from an expansive being.
Strive for wisdom at every juncture of your existence.
Like the Maasai, the long walkers,
Walk your talk.

Maasai do not lie; they will say everything to your face. This is a defining feature of the Maasai people, the values of respect, trust, and integrity.
– James Koileken, General Manager, Mara Simba Lodge, Kenya

After spending time at the drom market, we head off to tea. Yes, another tea ceremony with some nice bread, argan paste, and assorted fresh nuts. This is another one of those moments of solidarity.

LEADERSHIP RETHINK

Essential nomadic leadership qualities to embody:

Respect	Collaborate	Inspire
Trust	Communicate	Creative
Integrity	Clarity	Innovative
Walk your talk	Wisdom	Integrity
Truth	Intelligence of a nomad	Instinct
Consistent		Engagement
Congruent	Direct	Motivation

FINAL QUESTIONS

1. As a leader, do others refer to you as wise or having wisdom?

2. How do you think you can gain wisdom?

3. On your tombstone, or on departure from your organisation, how do you want to be remembered? As a leader who . . .?

DAY **8**

Remember: You Are Never Alone

Mission: to be instrumental is to build solidarity and unity

○

"Share! That's the key word, the word we can't avoid!"
– KEN BUGUL, SENEGALESE NOVELIST

JANUARY 8, 2018, SOUTHERN MOROCCO

T he Atlantic Coast that borders Morocco is serene and beautiful. I am at a lovely seaside restaurant up the coast from Sidi Ifni, watching the waves bashing up onto the sandy shore, leaving a white froth on the sand as the water retreats, a little like the froth on the top of the Moroccan tea. The January sun beats down brightly. My Berber friend, Aissa, and I are chatting over lunch about Berbers, nomads, tribes, their cultures, and at one point in the conversation he says, "You are never alone in Berber society; there is a form of solidarity."

I pause to reflect on his poignant words. Am I alone here by the ocean or is there solidarity with all parts of nature?

Sometimes you may feel you are alone in the expansiveness of the desert when it comes decisions you make, or the conversations you have, or your ideas are too far off for people to see or grasp and no one is behind you. You may feel weak, perhaps alone. At times like this you may think, *who can I speak to?* The hope is that the solidarity and alliances of your executive team and organisation will come together, and this can be assured through powerful top-down principles, trust, and interconnections.

Think back to the last chapter about gaining respect that leads to building trust—if you don't have this solidly built into your relationships, your solidarity will be compromised, and you just might feel you are going your path alone. Respect and trust leads to solidarity. Solidarity is a survival technique.

Nomads Believe in Solidarity

To go fast, go alone. To go far, go together.

– African proverb

Nomads go alone to explore at times and go together at times, such as when they all move at one time. When researching the definition of the word "solidarity," over and over, I encountered the word "unity" (Wikipedia 2019). It means to come together, to be bonded by societal ties.

In Mongolia or Morocco, or with the Maasai, while they may use different words to explain this social coming together and interdependence on each other, it all comes down to them believing in trusted solidarity or unity as a function of survival in their ecosystems or their social, business, and political communities. Their solidarity is strategic, focused, and together. Without the solidarity, it can be too dangerous to move to another destination without cohesiveness, trust, and connections within your clan or tribe and other external alliances.

You need the interconnections and networks to secure the roads you are travelling or to gather more information about people, situations, or the geographical direction ahead. In a corporation, it can be dangerous and risky to undergo an organisational change process, develop innovations, or convince your board of directors of a new vision unless you have cohesiveness backing you up. Why? Because you need the belief, respect, and trust of others. You need to know they are aligned and ready to support you in your vision. It is believing together—solidarity.

Solidarity Within Organisations

Aissa, who lives part time in Quebec, Canada, says when he goes back to Canada from the Sahara, he feels alone because where he lives in Southern Morocco, he says, "people always have time for you as they realise that solidarity is what makes them stronger." He believes western societies, in contrast, can learn to cultivate this solidarity of the Sahara. People do not trust each other in many of our societies today, and they live in fear.

What is the commonality between the desert and the sea? It is the immensity. There is the weakness of the people and the need for solidarity for survival. In the desert, you need a structure to follow to traverse the unknown immensity as the dunes will shift and change overnight; where you are today is not where you will go tomorrow. You need a structure to deal with the immensity and complexity of running an organisation and cannot have a selfish attitude about moving forwards. That is why solidarity is important. What you give is what you will receive.

1. In what ways does solidarity play out in your corporation?
2. Is unity important for you? Why?
3. What can you improve upon to develop more solidarity in the different departments of your company as well as with your strategic partners, customers, and even shareholders?

Steen Puggaard, Investor and Former CEO 4 Fingers Crispy Chicken, reflects on leadership in respect to structure and solidarity:

Every leader needs to be very honest with themselves and try to understand what they're good at and what they're bad at. They need to understand that they can't be everything; they need to augment their skills with a good team, and that team should not have the same skills but have complementary skills.

145

More often than not, the ego can get in the way of accepting solidarity because of many fears a leader or person may have surrounding not wanting others to know their weaknesses or vulnerabilities. There is absolutely no shame in vulnerability—it is a strength. What Steen is saying is to accept what you are good at and admit what you are not good at because there will certainly be someone who can fill your gap. Embracing this makes you not a weak leader but a strong leader as you are showing it is okay to not know everything. Some leaders do this but then fall down by not rewarding the knowledge or ideas of others. That comes back to respecting others, and by doing so, you will be respected, and solidarity is increased.

Arun Madhok, CEO Suntec Convention Centre, Singapore, suggested another way to keep structure and solidarity together while strengthening your team is to disrupt the status quo.

> I disrupt my team whereby I have everyone move every six months. Why? I do not want to create unnecessary tribes for the wrong reason; I want them to be created for the right reasons, i.e., projects, operations, etc., but not tribes that start warring with each other and having factions in the office. In order to grab the new, you must let go of the old. And if you have fundamentally spent all your time building this nest, you can't do it, it doesn't fit. Very often, the old just doesn't fit. For example, you can keep bringing in new furniture, and [if] at some point the furniture doesn't fit, and you need to let go.

A caveat to this approach is to keep in mind the different mindset typologies at play as not everyone will like those changes and will cause some challenges. You need to keep an eye on the solidarity and the team to keep moving towards the single goal with enthusiasm.

In what ways can you help and serve to bring greater solidarity to your teams and institution during these disruptive times?

Recognition Is Vital

Genoveva Ruiz Calavera, Director of the Western Balkans at the European Commission, likens solidarity to an orchestra:

> Any organisation is like an orchestra: if only the violins are recognized it's not good; it's [the combination] of all the music that comes out from the orchestra that has to be recognized.
>
> It is important you organize the organisation in a way that everybody can see their contribution into the great symphony come out, and that is

something many of the managers don't do enough. Everybody likes to be recognized in what you do, that it is for the greater good. You have to make sure that whatever the level of the person, they all get recognition and see that their contribution is important for the work the organisation is delivering.

It is also important to identify which [people] are not well placed. This is more difficult as it requires a lot of attention for the manager to notice the people that are not in the place where they are giving the best of themselves, and then they could become spoilers.

Solidarity comes from leadership that is clearly moving towards a vision, a purpose, or a goal and encourages and challenges you every step of the way towards the intended goal.

How are you challenging your executive team, managers, and employees to step up and be transparent about their strengths and weaknesses? What are you doing to help them move past their fears that challenge the existence of solidarity?

Solidarity Is a Strategic Exploration: Understand the Mindsets

> *Immensity is the desert, just like an organisation. There is structure in the desert nomads.*
>
> – Aissa Derhem

When a caravan sets off into the Sahara, the travellers need to be strategic about the journey because there are dangers along the way.

Everyone in the caravan is working towards the same goal and direction. It is an open structure. This is a structure where conversation, dialogue, and information sharing of those more knowledgeable about the path ahead is important. In nomadic cultures, greed or information withholding does not exist because they believe there is enough for everyone. These are your trusted partners, just like in business today.

Kwek Kok Kwong, CEO of NTUC Learning Hub in Singapore, believes one way of building structure leading to alliances and solidarity is through exploration, and in his function, it is through education. He feels,

> Nomads have the mindset of exploring because it is through exploration you can discover new opportunities, and now with all this transportation, it allows us to explore even further and faster. If you ask me how that

impacts our workforce in the future, I think they need to have an explorer mindset—they need to have a nomadic mindset—you must not be fearful about working either physically or exploring digital options. Increasingly, we want to expose our students to education that allows them to take risks and explore, and that's encouraging. It's about building the resilience, giving them that mindset of exploring.

Normally in corporations, this is the work of the Human Resources and Learning and Development Departments. Yet more often than not, those departments are ticking boxes that only go so far in developing solidarity through learning. They don't necessarily encourage by using the word "exploration" or have or understand this nomadic mindset. Just imagine if more had the nomadic mindset? What could this create?

Just imagine if more had the nomadic mindset?

Through research, I have found most people in the human resources or learning and development fields are of the builder and settler mindsets. This can create a status quo that is not where most companies want to be in Industry 4.0. This is where you need a solidarity linked to the vision, and you need to take into consideration the mindset typologies.

How important is it for you to understand the dominant mindsets of your leaders and managers in crucial roles? Why?

Sharing Is an Exploration

Sharing is integrated into the DNA fabric of nomadic communities. This is because if you are exploring and moving to new pastures, doing business in different geographical areas, or going to a land you are not familiar with, sharing information is vital. Think back to the tea ceremony described in Departure. Sharing information is one of the processes for building solidarity and gaining new alliances.

> That is why, when you meet
> another tribe or trader
> along the way,
> you stop,
> connect,
> engage,
> gather information,
> and share your information.

It is about
giving and receiving,
which is
a full circle
in their minds.

Anthropologically speaking, in old nomadic cultures, gaining these alliances with other tribes would involve intermarriage or merging businesses together under a like mind and direction. Such arrangements allowed for a larger network of alliances and trusted partners on the road ahead. This still exists in most societies, where people intermarry amongst large organisations, within royalty, or amid the celebrity circle. These are alliances that can build solidarity—not always for the good but sometimes for greed and power.

For nomads, there is a social contract created through values and respect for each other. In fact, you are protected by the social contract and context of these situations. Because of the solidarity and sharing of ideas, if a trader lies or tries to go behind someone's back or does a dirty deal, they will be no longer be in business. This is because the networks and alliances will spread the message rapidly, and, in relation to your company, you just might find yourself in bankruptcy.

In the Berber tradition, for example, if a business owner hires a person, they will train them to learn the whole business, so they know how everything works—from the processes and procedures all the way to the top. They prefer generalization rather than specialization. They are building solidarity or an alliance with this person; then, at some point, the business owner will tell the employee to go out on their own. The understanding and solidarity are that now they are interconnected, and when the other person builds their company, then they will do the same thing by training their people. The network, alliances, and solidarity grow.

> **" They prefer generalization rather than specialization**

Now, it is important to note that these alliances in nomadic cultures can also change, sour, and disintegrate. This is accepted as a way of being—they don't dwell on the split to keep their communities protected. This can also happen in organisations today, yet at times, revenge can occur, which is, in the nomads' view of the world, a waste of energy. You may think this is naïve in today's world, or you could flip it around and see how this may be the problem.

Another way leaders can illustrate a sharing culture is to walk their talk, communicate honestly, and be real. Steen Puggaard, Investor and Former CEO 4 Fingers Crispy Chicken, says,

I think to balance the cerebral aspects of leadership with the human aspects is very important. You've got to have a clear vision and a clear strategy for where the business is going. How you interpret and communicate [with] people, you need to make sure that you truly do it with some style. The important thing is being a real person, and that will create real people that are dedicated to the company's cause, or its purpose or its mission, and so on. And that's just the style that works for me—being real.

1. Ask yourself, are you sharing enough information with your executive team, shareholders, institution, or partners?
2. Do you promote sharing in your company? If so, how do you go about this?
3. Do you hold back information to increase your power?

Solidarity Needs Alliances

As in business today, so it is for the nomads traversing the Sahara in a caravan or the Mongols grazing the grasslands—you need protection in your migration while you explore. This protection (physically and mentally) provides a mutual benefit that comes through developing solidarity and alliances or partnerships.

You need alliances within your corporation and externally with strategic partners, companies you wish to merge with, or suppliers to shrewdly develop and grow. Growing and developing partnerships is the collaborative way forwards towards innovation, performance success, and growth for all. Alliances or partnerships can come about through outsourcing because it is more financially prudent to subcontract out areas of projects or innovation you don't have in-house. This can then lead to the smaller partner having access to a larger network, which is mutually beneficial for all.

As with the nomads, the trusted alliances will pave the way, which will benefit all.

1. What are the alliances you have within and without your organisation?
2. In what areas and for what reasons do you need to form alliances?
3. When was the last time you took a deep-dive look into your departmental operations and said, *we need alliances,* here or there?

One way of developing mutually beneficial internal solidarity is through talent recruitment. Kwek Kok Kwong, says,

One of the jobs of the CEO or MD is to make sure that you have an environment where this group can work together and not end up killing each

> other. So, recruitment is important. The second part is to create an environment where they can work together; in this sense, we thrive and survive together; we bring the organisation together to the next step forwards. Hence, understanding, communicating to, and hiring the right mindset for the right position [will] create the right mix of typologies considering the skills and tasks needed for the team to flourish.

Sometimes companies need to build solidarity and alliances within teams, and Steen shared a success case study, where he realised he needed to create the "vibe" in the company.

> What I realised was that my management team was working together, but they were not always getting along. I hired an executive coach that I've worked with in the past, and I said, 'Can you do a kind of a session for me and my small team of finance and marketing operations?' We did two, one-day sessions where we uncovered the 'me,' the 'we,' and the 'us' of working together.
>
> *No, no, no, it's very bad, this contentment* ”
>
> And one of the things I realised was that I was the only person who saw this contentment as positive work. They were all like 'No, no, no, it's very bad, this contentment.' [I said,] 'What do you mean? That's what drives this company, right?' I was able to account for them why I saw this contentment as something very positive, and they all now kind of get it. We see this contentment as the driver of, 'What else can we do?' and 'How can we do things differently?' That's relevant for a business in our phase of development because we're emerging; we're growing.

Creating Alliances with Mindsets

Another way of creating alliances that lead to solidarity is through the mindset typologies, whether you consider internal or external functions, communication, or team unity. Roland Genson, Director of the European Council, says,

> If you have a person with a nomadic mindset, [they] will never move a person with a settler mindset. In an organisation or public institution, those nomads are driving the change, and sooner or later the settler will eventually have to accept the change and be integrated into that change. However, between the settler and the nomad, you need a link as I think a nomad will not . . . convince a settler to follow him.

I think the builder is the link and understands the reasons to move and sees the value in this. The nomadic mind takes the strategic decisions to move and you need a builder to make the incremental changes to get there without disrupting everything at one time.

It is then the task of the leader to ally the right people to perform and communicate certain messages.

Creating Alliances through Education

Alliances come in many forms, especially when you travel to another country to help that country flourish. Genoveva Ruiz Calavera, Director of the Western Balkans at the European Commission, speaks about the challenges of the Balkans, which remains scarred by the wars of the 90s, but she is optimistic about the region's future:

What we are doing is working to enhance prosperity for the citizens of the Western Balkans. Linking the region to the EU and fostering its economic development is the most powerful tool to promote stability and reconciliation. We are investing, in particular, in communicating and engaging with the young people of the Western Balkans through educational programs and a digital agenda. They are a vector of change and can be our allies in anchoring peace in the region.

This concept of creating allies, alliances, solidarity, or unity is vital for moving forwards, whether you are a nomad in the Sahara (or the grasslands of Mongolia) or are a leader of a global company, government institution, or non-governmental organisation. It helps to bring people together to collaborate for a variety of reasons, internally and externally. It can also be positive or negative depending on the agendas being promoted or pushed. This concept can take the form of internal or external partnerships in marketing or advertising, product sales, digital outsourcing, or training programs, to name a few possibilities. The list is endless in nature.

1. How can you create alliances, internally and externally, that lead to solidarity in your teams and partners?
2. What alliances do you want to create to manifest more nimble or agile teams?
3. As a leader, what alliances do you want to forge to expand your organisation?

Connecting the Mindset Dots

Aissa Derhem, my friend from Sidi Ifni, Morocco, tells me as we eat lunch, "we need a nomadic mind to connect the dots." What dots you may ask? What works for nomads is the space to think and move, whether horizontally or vertically. This is a limiting factor for many corporate structures. Aissa suggests, when reflecting on companies today,

> The more space
> you have physically,
> mentally,
> emotionally,
> and creatively,
> the more ideas that you will have
> when sharing information,
> invoking
> a collaborative,
> organisational ecosystem.

Those are the dots of ideation, and it takes the solidarity of the nomad mindset to encourage this to happen. He feels that, more often than not, many organisations still want you to stay in your place or position, which limits self-expression.

He also helped me understand connecting the dots a bit better when he related nomadic cultures to the three mindset typologies. He said that "the settler mindset relates to those nomads that live in the oasis, and they are specialists in agriculture. They cultivate, don't travel, are tradespeople, and take care of the systems that are permanent in the oasis community."

we need a nomadic mind to connect the dots 🟧

On the builder mindset, he continues,

They take care of the alliances, the political structures, the infrastructure such as roads, water, and more. They have a width for open vision, and they can be the debaters and discuss options and decide not to go in a direction as it might not be the right time. They are the builders of the society. You need people with a nomadic mindset also, who are not staying in one place to make society and organisations' systems work. It takes all three mindsets and understanding what their qualities are and how they function, communicate, and relate.

The precaution here is that like attracts like. The same mindsets often attract each other. This can happen in recruitment where human resources, for example, might be settlers who will hire more settler mindsets because they fall into the "like" category, and they feel comfortable with the similar mindset. However, the position may not need that mindset. This is a normal behaviour because it happens unconsciously. Solidarity is recognizing and realising you need all three mindsets for the success of an institution.

When it comes to solidarity, unity, and cohesion, it takes wise leadership with big vision and the right mindset to connect the dots. Linda Locke, Branding Specialist, shares a personal story about misplaced loyalty from a CEO, which in many ways, led to disunity.

> We needed to change and stop being the way we were—you need someone who will just clean things up. Then I realised the global CEO was not watching it, and what happened was they left the senior guy too long, and so the clean-up person became the destroyer. They needed a nomad/builder (mindset) to come in. A big huge mistake was the company did not recognize what was going on [and] make the right moves at the right time. You see this happening a lot in business—they are filled with settlers (mindset) who were destroying the company, and the CEO is weighed down by loyalty to the settlers (his senior leaders).

Locke suggests that even though everyone has all three mindset typologies, the responsibility of a company falls to the leader or CEO. They need to know the type of mindset needed for different situations at different times or developmental junctures of a company. Being loyal to one group may not be what you need, and the leader has to make some tough decisions and be willing to approach the lion and risk their life for the betterment and solidarity of the corporation.

Connecting these dots is a form of solidarity in communities and institutions as every mindset typology is needed in some capacity to create unity or solidarity. This can then lead to forming alliances with strategic partners or stakeholders to grow your business faster.

You are never alone even if you feel you are 💬

The nomads do this, and companies of all sizes are doing this more and more. Take, for example, the different parts that go into building a car, an advertising campaign, or a unique digital program for educating the youth in the Balkans. You are never alone even if you feel you are. Look for and create solidarity, wherever you can, build trusting alliances, and exit when they are not trusting.

Unity is about organizing, creating something together, and sharing in order to stay together. I believe in unity and teamwork and the sharing of ideas—not just what I have.

– Lilian Naisola Maloi, Maasai, Mara Simba Lodge, Kenya

○

I leave my lunch on the Atlantic coast with Aissa with a feeling of solidarity not only with Aissa, but with nature as well. He helped me to connect the dots. You are never alone, and solidarity is about having the bravery and courage to act when necessary. Now to face the real powerhouse of leadership: how to Kill the Lion.

○ ○ ○

LEADERSHIP RETHINK

Essential nomadic leadership qualities to embody:

Solidarity	Sharing	Innovation
Alliance	Thriving	Mindsets
Exploration	Partnerships	Ecosystems
Strategy	Unity	Wholeness

FINAL QUESTIONS

When looking at your corporation from a distance, ask your honest self this:

1. How can I bring more solidarity and alliances, internally and externally, to my organisation?

2. What are the divisive factors, and how can they be changed?

3. What can true, honest solidarity do to the thriving ecosystems and success of my company?

Consider the Life of a Moran (Warrior)

Mission: to develop bravery and courage in your leadership

"You must be ready to learn how difficult this situation is—the difficult truth"
— BENSON KIPOLONKA MUNTERE

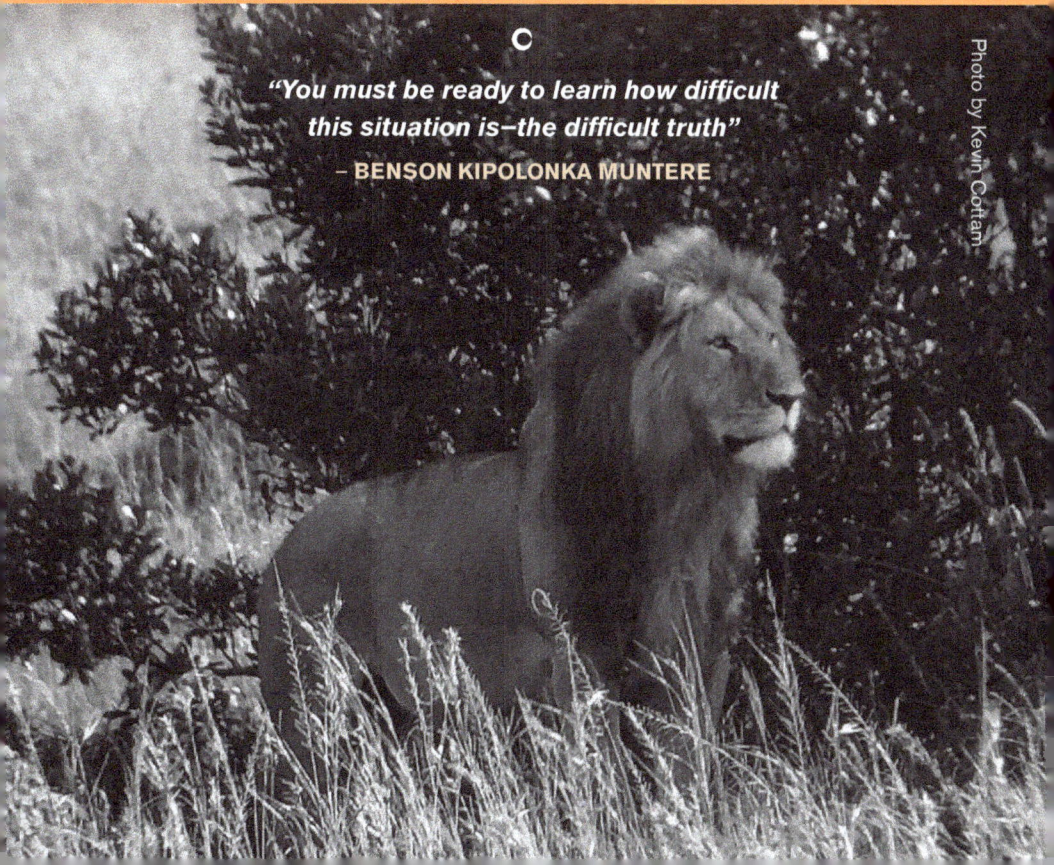

DECEMBER 20, 2017, MAASAI MARA, KENYA

Listening to my Maasai warrior friend Benson's calm, quiet, melodic voice fascinates me as he weaves together not only the history, but his experience of becoming a Maasai warrior and the obvious impact it's had on his personal development. I've been interested in this cultural tradition for years, especially the ritualistic killing of the lion, more mystically and romantically than logically or anthropologically, and now I am enthusiastically learning the real meaning of it.

The Maasai are peacekeepers. They are not a warring people—especially today. But they do have a rich ritual warrior history, and they have had to war with other tribes in Kenya.

*One note: While many indigenous and contemporary cultures today have rite-of-passage rituals for both genders, for the Maasai tribe, the warrior status was a coming-of-age ritual that was part of the migration to manhood.

This part of the Maasai Culture has been well documented by historians and anthropologists. It is an inspiring metaphor of strength, bravery, courage, strategy, tactics, and team unity that is paramount for contemporary leaders within corporations and governments and also for individuals, no matter the gender, race, culture, or religion.

Benson shares with me the hardships, tough rituals, and traditions of growth, knowledge, bravery, and courage that Maasai males from an early age went through in "the old days" (only about 10 years ago). It was said, "If you follow these different rites-of-passage stages to become a leader, you will be given the responsibility to protect the community, the families, and the clan.

When a young Maasai boy reaches around five years of age, he is sent daily into the pastures to herd and watch over the livestock: mainly cows, sheep, and goats. An older sibling may accompany him (typically, no more than five years older than the boy himself). They carry no weapons, only a herder's stick.

As they progress through boyhood, male Maasai youth endure various physical and mental hardships, such as teeth pulling, skin burning, tattooing, ear piercing, and the start of becoming a man through the circumcision process. Today, many of these rituals have ended due to education, religion, and simply change. However, circumcision to become a man continues. It is a ritual from childhood to manhood as it is in many cultures and religions around the globe.

Age Sets

There is a political and social structure within the Maasai culture that divides Maasai boys into age sets (or age groups), and an age set has a range of about five years (e.g., thirteen to eighteen). These sets are permanent, determined by the elder, and set for the life of the group. The groups' sizes vary but generally include between fifteen and twenty boys. The age sets will determine the hierarchy of grades, beginning with junior warrior and culminating in possible senior elder status. Each grade can last up to about fifteen years (http://www.bluegecko.org/kenya/tribes/maasai/agesets.htm).

In the next few pages, I dive into the various age sets in more detail to compare each stage of warriorhood to the layers and stages of corporate hierarchy.

Sipolio, The Initiation Stage (Newly Circumcised Youths Age 14 to 15)

Maasai boys are circumcised between fourteen- and fifteen-years-old, at which point they enter the sipolio age set: the first stage into warriorhood, which leads to manhood. The sipolio stage lasts for four or five months, during which time the sipolio go through a period of instruction to learn the arts of warfare and tactics. There are painful physical and mental challenges during this stage. These challenges are intended to build character, values, courage, and strength; during this phase, the elder guides and prepares them to be responsible people. It ends with a small ceremony.

The Corporate Sipolio

This initiation stage could be compared to when a person enters a new organisation or position. This can be challenging at first, learning new systems and cultures and forming new relationships; it can also be an exciting time. Hiring and onboarding serve as the initiation, no matter the position. When people enter companies, they are more often than not expected to have attained certain values, skills, and behaviours and developed their character and emotional intelligence so they are ready to launch into the learning curve of their new functions.

During this stage, a new employee might find it helpful to develop the nomadic qualities around solidarity: knowing they are never alone could help them adapt to their new situation more fully. Additional nomadic qualities to strive for include strong listening, stillness, remaining alert, and observing from a wide angle.

Think about your initiation into your company. What was that like for you?

Warriors, Stage 2 (Variable, from Age 15 to 23)

Following the sipolio stage, the Maasai enter into the warrior stage for up to five years, sometimes longer. The difficulties they face at this stage are having their knowledge, strength, courage, bravery, strategy, and respect tested all day, every day. Within this age set, there is only one level to complete at a time, and only when all members complete this stage (determined by the elder) is another level formed. As one level ends, another is created and the whole process starts again.

The final goal of this stage is to prove their manhood by killing a lion with nothing more than a spear 🍋

During this period, the boys are sent out into the forest for up to five years. During this time, they live off herbs, cow's milk, blood of the cow and meat from a slaughtered ox. They may also raid other livestock, capturing as many cows as possible. The final goal of this stage is to prove their manhood by killing a lion with nothing more than a spear. Once the boys have completed this stage, they go through a graduation ceremony, which leads into the next stage of becoming a senior warrior.

It is important to understand that not all warriors are heroes. Sometimes there are those who will back away from fighting and killing the lion or run away. In the Maasai world, this is classified as cowardice and holds a great stigma—they might not marry since, as a husband, they would not be respected or maybe even trusted; the community would likely look down on this person, and it would be a bigger challenge for them to prosper and elevate in the social system than those who killed the lion.

The Corporate Warriors

The warrior status in today's corporate world can be likened to one learning not only new roles and responsibilities for the position they were hired for, but all aspects of the company and even about themselves. This is when you gain a clear understanding of your dominant mindset, effective communication, how to deal with meetings in a strategic way, how to work in a team, how to make fast decisions, how to develop an entrepreneurial spirit, and so on.

Remember how some Maasai warriors back away from killing the lion? Are there people in your company who back away from negotiations or a performance review or even back down from what your shareholders are expecting of you?

Have a deep look at your talent development system and ask yourself if your early warrior stage is robust enough for the requirements of the company at this point in its development, such as how you embrace migration and expansion of the mind, seek the Foie Gras, develop unity, gain or earn respect (leading to trust), and other nomadic qualities.

Senior Warrior/Junior Elder, Stage 3
(After Age 23 and a Successful Lion Killing)

After having proven their bravery, courage, respect, and knowledge, Maasai warriors are allowed to marry, inherit properties, and start looking for jobs. The elder of the community will choose a leader from that age set, who more often than not, is the warrior who killed the lion. That person will become the junior elder. This duty is highly respected, and their role is to go to meetings and help solve problems or challenging situations in their communities.

The coming-of-age stages can be classified as levels of succession from the early stages to becoming a junior elder or a senior warrior. The succession is highly dependent on the senior elder of the clan. The senior elder will learn about the potential candidates from their heroics in the warrior stages. He will keep a keen eye on their knowledge, courage, strength, and resilience; their mental and emotional character and their ability to risk, change, adapt, and understand issues; and how they communicate and relate to others. Most importantly, the senior elder will watch how respectful they are of elders, youngsters, and others. Many factors go into deciding who becomes the next junior elder. The choice comes down to their mindset, spirit, and skill.

> *The choice comes down to their mindset, spirit, and skill.*

The Corporate Senior Warriors and Junior Elders

This stage in today's corporations can be linked to climbing the ladder towards the senior management and executive team. Here is where learning to lead becomes paramount. This happens by taking on major roles and responsibilities for growth, strategic planning and decision making, driving others towards the vision, or going forth as an expat in a different country. The roles could be compared to managers, directors, or higher depending on the senior leadership and the results.

Following these stages, the next level takes you to the executive team levels and the senior elder (or CEO in the corporate world).

Whether in the Maasai culture or companies of today, one can see similarities to the organisational hierarchical chart that determines the responsibilities of each level or position. Leaders are expected to acquire many of the nomadic qualities along the way, yet that doesn't always happen in reality. It takes a broadly thinking corporation with an expansive view to examine and encourage the development of nomadic qualities, and that in itself is nomadic. What is your corporation doing to encourage early selection for succession planning of your young leaders?

The most important tool, however, is taking the time to observe, listen, and question **"**

Many companies have robust leadership development programs like that of Tata, but from what I have researched, most institutions don't spend enough time or energy considering mindsets. They are obsessed with measuring everything about a person's performance and use a variety of psychometrics, assessments, and tools to do so. The most important tool, however, is taking the time to observe, listen, and question as that will get you closer to the mindset and spirit of an individual. Everyone can have the same skill level; however, not the same mindset or spirit that might be needed to fulfill their responsibilities effectively and efficiently.

I challenge you to look at your systems for developing or choosing your talent. What is missing?

Approaching and Killing the Lion

As Benson and I sit overlooking the Talek River, I notice there is a crocodile sitting on a sandbar in the river, its mouth wide open. Two baboons are sitting directly in front of the crocodile, staring at it, wondering—I am guessing—what strategically they should do. How would you respond to this crocodile? Nonchalantly, though watching in awe, my Maasai friend Benson and I gradually segue back to our conversation, leaving the baboon and crocodile standoff to play itself out.

He says,

I attended two lion killings, and you have to wait sometimes a long time for the lion. When the lion was noted, we divided into two groups to surround the lion so as to not give the lion space to flee.

Similar to what the crocodile was attempting to do with the baboons, I think.

In the warrior stage, your age set is all together, and it is about growing and working together for the survival of the group. It only takes one slip of not listening, or sensing, or gathering of information from nature and your colleagues and someone could get killed. Nature is raw, real and unforgiving. Nomads are interconnected with it, so they need to be still, listen, and be alert at the same time. There are those, of course, who are stronger physically and mentally than others; however, the age set is a team, and they need to support and bring those with less knowledge and ability along with them, so that they also become stronger, [more] courageous, and more knowledgeable.

Benson shared with me a tip that he learned when he was in the forest:

The elder told him, 'when you sleep, always sleep with your shoes on and your spears next to you. Put your blanket on your feet only and not over your head. You will need your ears to be open when sleeping to hear anything in nature that might be approaching.'

When you are in meetings or negotiations or walking the halls, do you (metaphorically) cover your ears?

Then Benson added, "You know through this process you will carry the heavy burden of protecting your families, your aging parents, and the elders and safeguarding the community."

❝ when you sleep, always sleep with your shoes on and your spears next to you.

Comparatively, in many ways, this training and great responsibility is like the military or security forces who protect our society. It could also be likened to the CEOs that guard their company's best interests and people or government leaders who put good policies (hopefully) in place for the benefit of their people.

Those in the senior warrior age set know the person who actually kills the lion becomes the bravest, and it increases his possibilities of leadership and love of women. Those are the rewards: recognition and being highly respected and trusted. They also know that each person in the age set has the potential to kill the lion, so there is a lot of competition and strategies to approach and kill the lion.

Speaking of rewards, this is often a hot topic in companies. People think rewards have to be in the form of money, and yet that is often not correct. What you see here from the Maasai is their rewards come through gaining recognition, respect, and trust. How can you inspire this practice of rewarding in your corporation?

The warrior(s) who get the most cattle are the most respected 🔸🔸

One example of the competitive nature of this journey is when the boys raid cattle. The warrior(s) who get the most cattle are the most respected. If warriors do not partake in the raid, they will not be as well regarded and will have less meat than the others. Bravery is tested all through the warrior phase in different ways, and the ultimate feat of bravery is confronting the lion and killing it.

Benson continues to teach me that the lion cannot be killed by one person. It takes the whole group to work together, and yet there will be only one winner; it is the support that is paramount for the survival of everyone.

This teaches us to remember we are never alone, which is a lesson that supports this quest of bravery and courage, just as we, in our corporate journeys, are never alone.

Intrigued, I listen as Benson continues his tale:

> Each of us must be brave enough to support each other, and you have to get close up as you cannot shoot when the lion is far away.
>
> When going for the kill, they will strategize and decide on the tactics they will use to surround and to approach the lion. You have to be very fast thinking and agile, and you have to act fast once you are in the hunt—and even stay ahead of your colleagues. We will first surround the lion in a circle so that the lion cannot get away. We then move closer and closer all together towards the lion, with each person being ready to rapidly approach and throw the spear. Then someone will break from the group and rapidly approach the lion and be the first to throw the spear, and others will rapidly follow suit. This is when we all take action to finish off the kill. If someone should become injured during the hunts at any time, they will be sent out of the group to heal.

He says these are the rules:

1. Be willing to sacrifice your life to go for the lion.
2. Be ready to learn how difficult this situation is, so that you can teach your brothers and sisters how difficult it can be.

3. Exhibit how strong you are, so you can strike the lion before your colleague.
4. Display with humility your fighting, strategic, and tactical skills.
5. Support each other because people can get killed in this fight. You must be prepared to run at the lion and not run away. That is a shameful act.

This reminds me of the tenacity necessary to achieve in today's culture. Think back to a negotiation or an important meeting. Can you see the similarities with killing the lion? Now reread those five rules I just listed above, thinking about that negotiation or meeting. Do you integrate them into your leadership style?

In the end, Benson shares,

> The first to kill the lion will take the hairy mane of the lion, which is a symbol of superb bravery. Our job is done; our warrior stage is over, and we come back to the clan, and we have gained incredible knowledge. Celebration is around the corner.
>
> After this period, our warrior phase is over, and we graduate into manhood. The hairy parts of the lion are exhibited to show [the] bravery of our age set and generation. This is a major learning for us, and the knowledge of life it brings is gained honestly.

Benson told me he was in two lion kills, and humbly stated he killed one of them. He admits that before he went through these two stages of life, sipolio and warrior, he had no idea what knowledge he needed in this world.

> It makes you stronger and stronger. It is the hunger for survival that is most important, and when you don't have the hunger, you are less knowledgeable.
>
> When we all accomplished the goals and our length of time in the forest was complete, we had marks on our bodies as if you have killed the lion. Traditionally, our bodies were covered in white dust like a tattoo as a symbol of the warrior. After graduating from that stage of life to manhood, your long, braided warrior hair was shaved off by your mother, and now you were able to take a wife, and you will be eligible to take on more leadership roles in the community.
>
> I realised how much more responsible I was to others, my age-set colleagues, and the pride that I had gained through this long process of self-development and survival. I really felt proud, as did the whole group, of the total understanding that if it wasn't for everyone in the group, we

❝ Traditionally, our bodies were covered in white dust like a tattoo as a symbol of the warrior

might not have been able to come back successful. The group support was so important in this process.

We believe that if you have not completed the challenges of the warrior phase, 'you know less because you have not encountered life's challenges.'

Respect is vital in our communities and it leads to trust. When we graduated, we were trusted by the whole society and community.

The Corporate Lion

Consider the lion as metaphor. Who, what, or where are the lions that appear or that you confront every day?

The lions in today's society, organisations, and governments have many different faces and meanings. Lions can be negatively experienced in conflictual ways such as an egocentric boss; a hostile merger; a micromanager; those with anger management and behavioral problems; a corporation buying up the competition; bullying governments; blaming, denying, or lying to others; new technology; or your thinking patterns. These are just a few examples of today's metaphoric lions or obstacles.

However, lions teach a warrior to see conflict as an opportunity to improve qualities such as strength, courage, tenacity, and decisiveness.

1. What are the lions you encounter outside of you?
2. What are the lions living inside your mind or body?
3. How do you confront these lions in your company, partners, competition, or life in general? What do you do, and what can you do to confront them mindfully?

The New Lion

The ritualistic tradition of killing the lion has since been outlawed by the Kenyan Government to preserve the lions and for other political and commercial reasons. Benson says, "you can kill a lion in self-defence and if your cattle are being attacked." The warrior status has now migrated to a completely different process: education. He says,

For you to be perfect in anything, you need to keep exercising [that skill.] To be perfect in school, you kill this lion that is found in classrooms; you need to kill this lion called higher marks, which leads to excellence by concentrating, sweating, and sacrificing. Nothing is given to you on a silver platter. When you are a warrior, you cannot be popular when you are seated like this (he gestures to his chair) until you sweat, you participate, and [you] go through the dangerous stages of war and lion killing.

In school, this is the same thing; you have to undergo different teachers until they learn you are a brave, strong, knowledgeable, and respectful person. Only then you will be chosen to lead the class challenges and situations so that people will find the respect for you. [When] people find something good in you, you will then be given a chance to be a leader. They will see that good thing in you [and you] will be given a chance. If you are bad, people will not see the good in you . . . if you are good , will see the goodness inside of you.

The old traditions have been lost, and this training of bravery, courage, knowledge, and strategy are metaphorically remembered through oral history, and now he sees these qualities being learned through education. He was one of the last age sets that went through the lion-killing ritual in his clan, and it is inspiring to see how he has migrated from the old traditions to contemporary life while still retaining the qualities of the warrior and the culture.

The Nomadic Spirit/Mindset of a Contemporary Warrior

How does learning about the cultural history of the Moran relate to today's nomadic spirit and mindset? As Jeremy Blain, Managing Director of Performance Works, says, "It's the will and the ability to fly."

I love this quote. It speaks to an environment that supports freedom, desire, purpose, and expansion, that is borderless and encourages an entrepreneurial and intrapreneurial spirit and mindset. It is allowing the warrior to expand, migrate, or change. As a leader, do you embrace this yourself? Or do you have many fears? Do you encourage the meaning of the quote when considering processes, systems, management, and personal development within your company? Here is a case study that brings forth this metaphor and learning.

Michael Teoh, Millennial Entrepreneur: Nomadic Spirit versus Mindset

Since I've been talking about coming-of-age rituals in this chapter, I'd like to share some thoughts from a millennial entrepreneur I met in Kuala Lumpur. I met Michael Teoh, the brainchild behind Thriving Talents, when I shared the stage with him at a speaking engagement.

Michael has much wisdom given his young age (26) when it comes to human development, large institutions, and leadership. He understands the nomadic mindset fully. From speaking to him and watching him, he reminds me a little of Benson with his warrior spirit and mindset.

> The difference between spirit and mindset is that spirit is rather intangible; you can always encourage yourself to say 'I need to change, I need to innovate, I need to learn, I need to benchmark,' but when you talk about nomadic mindset, this is when you need to take the intangible spirit you have to plan it out and put it into the tangible.
>
> *I need to change, I need to innovate, I need to learn, I need to benchmark*
>
> So, what happens when people who claim to have nomadic spirit . . . may not have a nomadic mindset? Sure, you know there's a need for you to change, you know there's a need for you to reimagine, [to] challenge yourself. Is this the best product or service that you could do? I know it has served you well for the past twenty to thirty years, but right now it is the twenty-first century, [so] how are you going to change?
>
> CEOs, leaders, entrepreneurs may always lie to themselves, saying that 'I want to change, I want to change.' They may have the spirit, but are they changing? Are they making plans? I believe you must be willing to take risk; you think about taking risk when you are in a nomadic spirit, but when you are in the nomadic mindset, you need to ask yourself, 'are you willing to take risk?' If so, commit to taking that risk.

The spirit, the mindset, and the risk Michael is speaking about here all link back to the Moran coming of age of sipolio and warrior youths. The stages not only develop the strength and courage of the Moran to kill the lion, but they can also be linked to developing the entrepreneurial spirit needed today in corporations. There is an interdependence on others, the team of others in your age set, which links to the performance, producing tangible results. For the Moran, the ultimate goal is not only killing the lion, but gaining respect and building trust. What is extremely important in these small groups is their reliance on others, and for this you must be honest, vulnerable, and strong at the same time because the survival and success of the group is the first priority.

Michael says,

> To me, a nomadic company is a company willing to take risks to explore greener pastures to be innovative and to know that settling in one market,

settling on one thing that they do extremely well, is not enough, especially when they are faced with adverse competition.

Having a nomadic mindset means having the courage to go out there and ask for help from people, admitting to yourself that your company, your business, may be the market leader, but do you have the courage to face your ego and go out there and talk to people?

Michael's words mirror the life of a Moran: risking, asking for help, recognizing that competition exists within your fellow Morani, and truly believing. Another quality of this development stage or the nomadic spirit is truth.

> **Maasai do not lie; they will say everything to your face**

As James Koileken, General Manager of the Mara Simba Lodge and a Maasai, told me, "Maasai do not lie; they will say everything to your face. This is a defining feature of the Maasai people: the values of respect, trust, and integrity."

1. What if your mindset mirrored that of a Moran?
2. What would you do differently?
3. How would you promote this way of being in your organisation?

Mentoring in the Way of the Moran

In corporations today, there is considerable energy spent on the generation gap and the coming together of multiple generations. How can we bring them together? Consider looking at it another way, where the millennials represent the sipolio/junior levels mentored by the senior elders. Mentoring is highly encouraged today in some companies, yet still not in most. Ask yourself why not.

The coming-of-age stages in the Maasai culture can be adapted to your organisational mindset. Again though, to see this relationship, you need to not only have the nomadic spirit Michael speaks about, but also have the temerity to put it into tangible action.

Change Has Happened

The Maasai are embracing the changes—some faster than others—because they see the world around them is changing rapidly, and they will need to find new pastures to provide for their families and communities. Some are leaving their family *enkang* or *manyatta* (village) for urban dwellings and jobs. Education is becoming the new warrior ritual. This is good if their adaption carries forwards their redeeming nomadic qualities and outlook on life.

I could see the emotions in Benson's eyes when he spoke about the nomadic mindset and the changing times.

> It is [more] difficult than it was then. There [is] a moment when you cannot see with your own eyes. It is very difficult to see or experience, which is leaving people in a dilemma. It was beautiful, but it is ending. Today, you want education, you want a job, so that you are able to stand for you parents, children, and friends. When you have not gone to school, you must change, you must shift to compete with the world, compete with the current life.'

The fundamental warrior qualities that have resonated for generations within the nomadic cultures and contemporary societies of today are resilience, courage, bravery, strategy, and growth. They are still vital for survival today, only in a different way.

Consider how these nomadic rituals parallel the intentions of today's contemporary societies when it comes to the educational system and employee growth. When grooming talent for higher positions within your company, what qualities and mindsets are needed to excel?

> *When I graduated to manhood,*
> *I was different.*
> *I feel I am now one of the important people in the community*
> *who has gone through the challenges.*
> *I feel brave,*
> *strong,*
> *knowledgeable,*
> *a tactician,*
> *strategic,*
> *have the ability to stand firm, take the lead, and be bold,*
> *and I am a person who*
> *thinks fast.*
> *I realise now*
> *a lion cannot be killed by one person;*
> *it takes the whole group.*
> *I am a parent now and have*
> *responsibilities for others.*
> *We are migrating . . . where we were is not where we are . . .*
>
> – Benson K. Murtere

After parting with Benson that day, I realised how much I had learned about the fundamentals of leadership and life. I began to wonder what lions are inside and outside me that I want to confront. What about you?

○

Your journey to discovering the leadership qualities of the nomadic mindset has gifted you with rich stories of insightful wisdom passed down through the centuries. As in every physical or metaphorical journey, you are ready to migrate home, or to your newly expanded destination, with deeper awareness of you and your institution.

○ ○ ○

LEADERSHIP RETHINK

Essential nomadic leadership qualities to embody:

Bravery	Tactics	Risk
Courage	Responsibility	Leadership
Strength	Leadership team	Knowledge
Insight	Unity	Succession
Resilience	Agile	Growth
Strategy	Intuition	Mentorship

FINAL QUESTIONS

What if you were to step back right now and reflect upon the last time you were a warrior and you confronted the lions inside or outside your corporation or in your own mind?

1. What would a nomad do differently in this situation?

2. How would you confront, respond to, and communicate with yourself and others?

3. What are the ways, practices, or interventions you can use to inspire the qualities of a warrior in you and your organisation?

RETHINK

PART 4

Destination

○

"It is the land that ultimately owns the man"

– MOSSI ORAL TRADITION

Photo by Orgil Batsaikhan

A Destination is but a pause before you begin your journey all over again. A Destination is like a goal or an outcome, if you may. In this pause, realise there are three Destinations that are the result of the past Discoveries you've just experienced. Your leadership and your organisation's survival and ability to thrive depends on a strong corporate culture, the ability to sustain a sustainable world view, and the reminder to Never Settle . . . for Too Long, otherwise you will become a dinosaur. The three Destinations are "the land that ultimately owns the man (human being)."

Believe: Culture is a Pillar

○

"A man without culture is like a zebra without stripes"
– MAASAI ORAL TRADITION

DECEMBER 20, 2017, MARA SIMBA LODGE, KENYA

"I love and believe in my culture," says Lilian Naisola Malo, a majestic Maasai woman in the Maasai Mara, Kenya.

Lilian is standing at the reception desk of the Mara Simba Lodge when I arrive to check in. She is a tall, statuesque woman who speaks precisely and slowly with clear English, wears an earth-coloured Lodge uniform, and wears her long, pitch-black hair up in many fine, intertwined braids. She greets me with a wonderful smile, and we instantly strike up a conversation. I ask her if she has time while I'm visiting to chat with me. She nods her head.

Four days later, we finally sit down to have a conversation. I sensed from the moment I met her that something was different about Lilian, and I was right. Lilian is a single mother with two children and is bringing them up alone. She never married and has no intention of doing so in the future. She adamantly shares, "I am the breadwinner and will support my children." This is unusual in the Maasai culture as historically marriage is the only path forwards.

I am the breadwinner and will support my children

Lilian tells me her upbringing was different than most Maasai women because of her father's diverse mindset. Her father is an educated man. Again, that is unusual for Maasai men. What often happened in the old days—perhaps twenty or thirty years ago— was if a male was not a good herder or was not toeing the line, they were sent to missionary-like schools to be educated as a punishment. Because of his education and expansive outlook on life, he brought Lilian up differently than other Maasai women. He encouraged her to be educated and receive advanced diplomas. This she did.

When we speak about her social culture, she says it is changing with the times, "We are evolving, migrating." When she speaks about family gatherings that she doesn't attend much because of the other women, I can see the sadness. Traditionally, the woman takes care of the children, and if you are not married, you are not respected. As you learned in Day 7, respect leads to trust, and it is a highly regarded cultural quality, not only for the Maasai, but perhaps for all cultures.

Lilian says, "When we have family gatherings, the women ask me to play with the children because they treat me as one of the children." Therefore, she prefers not to mingle with them. She says it is hard to be a single woman in their culture and be respected.

Yet, she appears to be a confident, strident, young woman with clear, educated, and expansive contemporary views, opinions, and beliefs about what she wants in life. At the same time, she seems relaxed about her destiny. Lilian continues to talk about leadership she admires, and she is so happy that female leaders are stepping up and taking on powerful roles in Kenyan society and in their traditions, their aspirations in life, their politics, and of course, their culture.

I can sense she loves her culture even though she has misgivings about the way she can be treated. She continues to glow when she speaks about the Maasai people and their qualities and beliefs, their history and current changes. It seems she is able to put family problems aside and be strong, bold, and courageous. Lilian takes things in stride just like a warrior would do. She says, "Culture is what binds us together and is vital for survival. No matter what, we will die for our culture."

1. Would you die for your ethnic culture?
2. Will you go to bat for others in your corporate culture?
3. How important is developing a strong culture in your company?

Culture is . . .

Culture can be a tough thing to explain. "Culture" is one of those words like "values" that is thrown around without much understanding of the meaning. Cultures are energy: alive, thriving entities that flow and exist in the deepest cellular level of the human condition.

Of course, culture can mean different things to different people, yet people generally have a consensus of opinion. For the purposes of this book, culture is too massive a subject to deeply tackle; therefore, I am going to confine the meaning, as I have been doing, to mindset, where it pertains to individuals and organisations.

Lilian and the Meaning of Social Culture

In Lilian's story, what she is speaking about, according to the Merriam-Webster (2018) definition of "culture," is "the customary beliefs, values, constructs, social forms, and material traits of a racial, religious, or social group." The challenges she is facing within her culture is that she has evolved and migrated to further expansion through her education and thinking patterns rather than yielded to the more traditional beliefs upheld by the tribe. This is causing a clash of ideologies, yet she is accepting and adapting to the new realities of today while keeping the fundamental culture of the Maasai deep within her. Lilian is finding new destinations by migrating to a more expanded view of the nomadic mindset: her innate mindset.

The Meaning of Social Culture in Organisations

For organisations and institutions, the Merriam-Webster (2018) meaning is, "the set of shared attitudes, values, goals, and practices that characterizes an institution or organisation."

What organisational culture do you seek? How is your culture created and lived? Who sets the culture up? How do you inspire it to evolve, migrate, and adapt over time? Do you shape it from the top down or through employee consensus?

If you don't shape the culture of your corporation, then the people within it will, unconsciously. It is especially important when you are experiencing a growing diversity of employees who are more nomadic in their ways of being and come from multiple, diverse socioeconomic and cultural heritages. This mixture greatly influences the overall culture of the organisation.

What is the culture of your institution? Can you describe it or put it into pictures, words, or actions?

Organisational Culture: Shifting Mindsets

Due to the evolution in societies, organisations, and industrialisation where there is an overlapping migration from the digital revolution (Third Industrial Revolution) to the Fourth Industrial Revolution (Industry 4.0) of artificial intelligence and biological technologies, social and organisational cultures are having to adapt on many levels. Your thinking patterns regarding solution making, creativity, management, and leadership are not the mindset needed for the future. This leads to changing mindsets.

You won't understand other cultures unless you listen and have a curiosity 🙶

This is where the nomadic mindset holds credence when compared with the other mindsets you have and need in your organisational culture (nomadic, builder, and settler). This is a new destination, traversing the migration to expansion from the Third Industrial Revolution to Industry 4.0 with more fluidity. Is it a challenge? Yes, yet all challenges are opportunities in disguise—remember the Foie Gras.

A friend and expansive thinker, Tim Love, former Vice-Chairman and CEO Asia Pacific India Middle East and Africa Omnicom Group, explains, "The nomadic mindset becomes rather interesting when it comes to listening to other cultures. You won't understand other cultures unless you listen and have a curiosity." Listening and curiosity. Sound familiar? Two powerful qualities discovered in Day 2, Adopt the Anatomy of a Bird. Let's dig a bit deeper.

Listen, See, and Become Curious

To understand what is happening in your corporation, it is important to reflect on the diversity of societal cultures and the mix of the different mindsets (nomadic, builder, and settler). There are two things to consider. One is that all things (systems) are interconnected, and the second is that migration to expansion, or being more "extra-environmental," is necessary.

> **Think vastly;
> act narrowly.**

Companies are part of the seamless weave of nature, not apart from it. Leaders, shareholders, and Wall Street more often than not don't seem to think they're part of this seamless weave. If you consider your culture as being a reflection of and interconnected to the whole (internal and external environments), this will assist in leadership, performance, and building power in your inner organisational culture—and it will reflect positively on your bottom line. This will help you craft the organisational culture you desire.

On this note, Tim taught me much about what he'd learned of anthropological and organisational culture on his leadership journey in advertising and marketing through the major transformations of the industry in the digital age. Something he learned from Howard Gossage piquéd my curiosity because it directly relates to migrating to expansion as well as to what my student friend from the National University of Mongolia, Binderiya, said "Think vastly; act narrowly."

Back in the late 1960s, Howard Gossage was a superb copywriter and a leading voice in the advertising industry. Articles he penned such as "Is Advertising Worth Saving?" and "Is There Any Hope for Advertising?" explored the evolution advertising and communications was experiencing with the proliferation of television media globally. Gossage said, "In order to communicate in the emerging world of electronic media, you need to be extra-environmental."

He went on to say,

> Creativity is a process that gets its start when we become aware of our environment. Awareness is becoming conscious that there is something bigger controlling us than we had thought. It requires an ability to think outside of what is right before us.

To explain this, Tim shares a story that Gossage used:

> Let us suppose that an ant has lived all his young life inside an anthill. He is not really aware that the anthill is his one and only world as he doesn't know anything else. So, one day they send him off on an important assignment: to drag back a dead beetle, say. He goes outside the anthill. Two things happen: 1) He sees the anthill for the first time; 2) He becomes aware

that the world is a very big place. Does this mean that he is aware of his environment? No, because what he doesn't know is that the anthill is inside a greenhouse. The only way he'll become aware of the greenhouse is if he goes outside of it. And, even then it won't do him much good, because, you see, the greenhouse is inside the Houston Stadium, and so on.

This comes back to thinking extra-environmentally, which is seeing with an expanded view of a situation or from a vast distance, like the Eye of a Hawk before you focus in on the solution.

This relates to where we are today with regards to developing an interconnected culture for Industry 4.0. What is being said here is you need to seek the expansive thinking of a nomadic mindset, have the Eyes of a Hawk, then take a chance on the different possibilities and opportunities that might be presented to you. These are cultural beliefs, values, and qualities you might want to embrace yourself, if they're not already part of your organisational culture.

Lilian from the Mara Simba Lodge in Kenya is already doing this within her own social culture while living firmly in her nomadic mindset.

1. How are you seeing, listening, and understanding your leadership culture from an extra-environmental point of view?
2. Are you thinking extra-environmentally or migrating to expansion? Can you do more?
3. What is the framework that is going to get you to your desired cultural destination?

What can help you is to start listening more, become more curious by seeing what is out there, and begin to fully understand the impact of interconnectivity. Ask yourself, *what would a nomad think or do*?

Case Study: Clearasil

When Tim went to Europe the first time, he went around to 26 Omnicom Group offices in 26 countries. He noticed each one handled Clearasil, which is a product targeted at young people. The creative people wanted to present him with their Clearasil work. Why? Because their Clearasil work was focused at the population of young indigenous teens and was more modern in execution. This meant the creative people had more leeway to create than they did with other products such as an adult-targeted product like laundry soap or motor oil.

He came back from his trip having seen a multitude of different creative approaches being used across the region. When Tim returned home to Brussels, he found his three children watching cable television. He noticed they were watching music videos on MTV, but they kept switching channels to other MTV channels from different countries throughout Europe every time a commercial came on.

Since MTV had a strong teen audience everywhere, Clearasil and their chief competitor, Oxy 10, from GlaxoSmithKline, had invested heavily in advertising on MTV across the region. Tim could see the logic in this tactic because his kids would watch a few seconds of the commercials before switching to other MTV channels.

Each time a Clearasil commercial came on a different MTV channel, he saw how disconnected the Clearasil brand was given the wide variety of music, character, and tone used in each country; whereas, the Oxy 10 commercials from each country were totally unified in presentation, brand, and copy.

Tim could easily see Oxy 10 was eating them for lunch, as he put it, with their strongly coordinated approach and bold Oxy 10 narration read by the same announcer in each country. Teens across the region were getting a consistent brand impression about Oxy 10, even when accounting for the language and visual differences in each country. His colleagues working on Clearasil were operating in the limited frame of reference of their own teens and local MTV (thinking narrowly). Yet their target audience was looking beyond the local MTV channel (extra-environmental and expansive). And simultaneously, teens were increasingly sharing their ideas and preferences on a host of issues across borders due to the rapid advance of the worldwide web and growth of social media platforms such as MySpace, Facebook, and YouTube.

> **" It is important to understand where your people are coming from**

In other words, unity in your message across all departments and units, horizontally and vertically, creates stronger potential to develop a culture aligned towards your overall vision (remember the cheetah from the Eyes of a Hawk).

It was then that Tim's frame of reference as a leader changed.

Since then, Tim has continued to draw relationships between nomadic qualities, behaviour, and corporations. When you study this case, you can start to see certain proclivities of nomadic thinking and nomadic behaviour. It is important to analyze what characteristics influence nomadic thinking, particularly when you are evaluating integrated solutions across borders or talent on a team. It is important to understand where your people are coming from. This then leads to creating the corporate culture you need for Industry 4.0.

Achieving Interconnected Culture through Mindset

What might then be some of the characteristics or qualities that influence interconnected culture? This leads directly back to the nine days of Discovery where you experienced, through stories, the culture qualities and behaviours underlining the nomadic mindset, where social culture meets organisational culture.

Mindset as Capital

One way to achieve interconnectivity is to understand the breadth of the quote by Binderiya, a student at the National University of Mongolia: "Mindset is your capital." This doesn't require much explanation, but for Mongolians, it means that successes and actions are due to mindset. Mindset is your currency in life: positively and negatively. For example, if you have entrepreneurial spirit (nomadic) and you lack creativity, your business may not flourish

Mindset is your capital 🙶

with new ideas. Alternatively, if your main focus is numbers, quarterly returns, and a build, build, build mentality (builder mindset), you potentially won't see the bigger picture. And if you don't like taking risks yet want to move up the ladder, then your settler mindset might work against you. To combat this, you might start with asking yourself what a nomad might think or do in these situations?

For a culture to thrive, you want to have the right mindsets in the right positions at the right time migrating, aligning, and adapting to the vision. A sustainable future comes from understanding, being interconnected, and allowing all the parts and systems (including people) to function freely. While this takes many things, flexibility and being extra-environmental or migrating to expansion are key factors of success.

Dominant Mindsets of Leaders Today

On this point of mindset and leadership, I became curious and asked Dr. Tanvi Gautam, C-Suite Advisor and Executive Coach, her opinion of the dominant mindset of leaders today. She believes "the majority of leaders today fall into the builder mindsets who are trying to be nomads." She also adds that she knows very few nomadic leaders, and her specialty is working with top leaders all over Asia, male and female. From my research as well, it seems some organisations don't know what to do with this free-thinking, creative approach that appears in a nomadic mindset.

Considering some of the challenges leaders might have, Tanvi says,

It is crucial for leaders to have the agility to move between mindsets and be mindfully aware of this. It takes a high-level awareness to know when to switch, and I am not sure if leaders have this capability."

This is where a nomadic mindset can help enormously, and the best leaders, Tanvi finds, are "those that can switch back and forth between mindsets with ease, but first you need to be acutely aware of your dominant mindset plus the dominant mindsets of others."

Mindsets are interwoven into the culture of your corporation and play a role in manifesting how your culture functions (if you need to refresh your memory about the qualities associated with the mindsets, refer back to the last section of Part 2, Departure 3: Recognize the Nomadic, Builder, and Settler Mindsets).

1. What happens to a culture driven by leadership that is settler-mindset focused?
2. What happens to a culture driven by leadership that is builder-mindset focused?
3. What happens to a culture driven by leadership that is nomadic-mindset focused?

Roland Genson, a Director at the European Council, says,

> Leaders will need a nomadic mindset because it is moving all the time. They have to give this stability—this reference [of], 'you can trust in me because I know how to deal with this change, because for me, change is normality.' I would never follow a settler, who for the first time in his life, would have to drive a change process. You have settlers who are intelligent people but not comfortable with change, and they say, 'I have to change this service,' and they will go through the change as a settler, really not at ease [doing] this.

What mindset does your organisational culture need right now to thrive?

Developing a Corporate Culture that Embraces Failure

Besides developing a mindset that embraces being extra-environmental, migrating to expansion, and "thinking vastly; acting narrowly" as part of your corporate culture, encouraging failure can stimulate your employees to grow and learn. Refer back to what anthropologist Romain Simenel said, "They (nomads) have this strength to always transform a fatality into an opportunity." On this note, Tim Love, formerly of Omnicom Group, shared his views on this valuable leadership mindset quality: failure.

> One of the fundamental things in leadership is to create an environment, a culture, where people can fail in the quest for learning without being penalized forever. The reason is, in an organisation, when we are successful, [we] repeat what we have just done; we are almost superstitious about it. And

this is good business when you are successful with something to maximize it by being more efficient and just replicating [that] set of circumstances. But the business environment and strategy is dynamic, so replication can leave you vulnerable if you don't marry it with sufficient innovation.

Culture is always evolving; trial and error and failures along the way lead to innovation, if you allow it. Tim continues, saying,

Innovation is creativity that is realised. Creativity for creative reasons is only creative. It only has value when the creativity has an effect or is realised. Only when creative ideas are realised [does] it manifest itself as innovation. I think what is important about leadership and the three different typologies (nomadic, builder, and settler) is how to encourage a sufficient level of nonreplication and experimentation. With experimentation comes high risk because experimentation as opposed to doing what was being done before can lead to failure.

You need to make the rules clear: what are the consequences of failure?

Leadership should encourage experimentation and learning. If that doesn't take place, the natural tendency of your company will be to replicate what was done before, and that's a built-in negative in a dynamic marketplace. Tim says you learn more from your failures than your successes, but he adds a caveat, "You need to make the rules clear: what are the consequences of failure?"

Tim's Recipe for Saluting Failure

- Talk about the problem privately.
- Encourage your employees to fail, and if they do, speak up about it, don't hide it.
- In situations where they wanted to make a point and it failed, applaud them, then have a discussion to find out what they learned.
- People won't experiment if they know they are going to be punished for trying something (Same as *frapping* the camel!). On the other hand, they must know they are going to be punished if they continue making the same mistake over and over again. Be clear when communicating this.
- Encourage people to come to you to share their results. Then throw it back at them and ask, "What are we learning from this, and how can we do this differently in the future?"
- It is important to promote thinking in different ways.

- Reward experimental ideas.
- Reward collaborative ideas and divergent thinking.

Tim says, to develop a thriving corporate culture, you need to reexamine and promote the qualities of a mindset: a way of thinking.

1. What corporate culture do you wish to create?
2. What qualities, behaviours, and mindset do you want in your people that will help define the culture?
3. How will you go about encouraging and inspiring them?

Creating a thriving culture is a destination, and it is always evolving, changing, and migrating.

Destination: Culture and the Intelligence of the Nomad

Remember nomad means "the movement of the mind." Think of your institution as a brain with many minds: it is never static, and there is an interconnected dynamic flow of the mindsets. This is a destination of your organisational culture. Keep it migrating it to expansion from place to place to discover greener pastures. This is the cultural destination you are seeking.

Lilian Naisola Maloi from the Mara Simba Lodge in Kenya loves her culture, even though she isn't always fully part of it. However, her nomadic mindset, which is part of her culture, runs in her veins and is an ever-evolving destination. What destination and backbone do you want for your corporate culture? Are you willing to think interconnectively and extra-environmentally, while seeing, listening, and understanding the mindsets that make up your culture?

> **Remember nomad means "the movement of the mind."**

Believe me, culture is a pillar that draws people and clients to you. The right culture with the right mindset can encourage, motivate, and inspire belonging and performance. It can bind people together. Culture is your decision and creation to develop.

Once you have developed the culture, be flexible and let it evolve. Do you have the ability to sustain your culture through your actions, words, and deeds? Your next destination is sustainability.

Culture is the possibility to create, renew, and share values.
It is the oxygen that enhances humanity's vitality.

– Jacques Nanema

○ ○ ○

LEADERSHIP RETHINK

Essential nomadic leadership qualities to embody:

Culture	Leadership	Dynamism
Interconnection	Communication	Flow
Wholeness	Vision	Flourish
Organisations	Listen	Grow
Behaviours	Curiosity	Evolve
Beliefs	Extra-environmental	Change
Perspective	Perception	Environment

FINAL QUESTIONS

1. What is your dominant mindset as well as your organisation's?

2. Can you specifically explain to anyone what your corporate culture is?

3. What are some ways you can develop your corporate culture more proactively?

Integrate:
The Ability to Sustain, Sustainability

The ability to sustain, sustainability,
is the ability to weather time, accept the changes,
protect our resources for longevity, and realise that every part
of the universal food chain plays an intricate, crucial, major role
in what makes the world go 'round: an interconnected universe.

C

"We cannot solve our problems with the same thinking
we used when we created them"
– ALBERT EINSTEIN

DECEMBER 20, 2017, MAASAI MARA, KENYA

Joel Soit, my Maasai brother, picks me up from the Mara Simba Lodge for our morning-long walk through the barren grasslands of the Maasai Mara. While we chat, stopping at times to listen to the birds singing, watch the baboons frolic, or focus on our ultimate quest to find the hiding place of the shy hippos, I happen to mention the ground looks barren, and he just smiles. Then he says . . .

"Lions killed two of my cows last night." This stops me in my tracks. Fear rises inside me with concern for the safety of the young herders. He says the herders are okay. We look each other in the eyes, and I feel his calm, still presence. It seems, from his matter-of-fact statement, that it has no real effect on him. This helps calm me. I sense this a normal part of existence in the Mara. It is just like the cup of coffee I had for breakfast—a normal occurrence—that's just life in nature. However, I know it bothers him to some extent because every cow is currency for sustaining their survival, and now he has two less.

Lions killed two of my cows last night **"**

We continue our walk, talking from time to time while looking for the hippos. Walking in the stillness of nature gives me time to reflect upon this lion-and-cows situation and observe more of the nomadic existence and how they sustain themselves on a daily level.

Joel stops at a tree and rips off a branch, then puts it in his mouth to take the bark off one end. He chews the wood at the end to fray it and then moves the branch around in his mouth like a toothbrush. "This is how we brush our teeth," he says. He hands me a branch, and I repeat his actions. To my surprise, it feels great and my teeth feel cleaner.

These two examples, the killing of the cows and the toothbrush tree, exemplifies their innate ability to sustain their existence in different ways. Even the shy hippos who are afraid of humans are hiding somewhere, and that is how they hope to sustain their existence. Life is raw for nomads, and they strongly believe that to sustain the world, the world needs to embrace and be responsible for the interconnectivity of all things.

The nomads' ability to sustain their culture and be resilient for thousands of years is a result of sharing, taking risks, observing threats, fast thinking, vision, stillness, community, culture, family, adaptability, flexibility, and being ready to migrate—not just physically but mentally. All are qualities of the nomadic mindset.

This story is just part of nature's magical play. How does nature's play translate into sustainability for you?

Sustainability is . . .

Sustainability is the interconnection of four pillars: people, planet, profit, and culture. The right balance of all four creates the circle of life. These pillars are in constant migration, ever changing, ever flowing, and definitely not static. The same goes for what your leadership, corporation, clients, and markets ought to be, theoretically.

There is an innate, flowing, natural balancing and rebalancing act that allows harmony of all parts. The hazard to watch for is when unbalance occurs in such things as understanding, vision, clarity, leadership, market disruption, and more. That is why the leader needs to be bold, strong, and aligned to their true north, i.e., vision, or direction.

Sustainability is a destination for many leaders around the world today. To want or have the ability to sustain is another destination to strive for and is interconnected to fulfilling your business model. This sometimes is a challenge for many leaders and individuals because they might be limited by shareholders, fiduciary matters, boards of directors, the executive team, or even clients and different viewpoints. The other side of that coin, though, is your personal courage, beliefs, and values to drive a company in a purposeful direction for all of mankind. It may sound lofty; however, this is vital today for future generations.

> **❝ Sustainability is a destination for many leaders around the world today**

It takes the right mindset to understand all three mindsets—nomadic, builder, and settler— are needed to work together to sustain all systems, whether personally or corporately. Your leadership requires the intricate balance that is sustainability and knowledge of the mindsets.

Is sustainability a destination for your organisation? Is it part of your vision, mindset, and business model? It should be if you don't want to become a dinosaur. What do you have to do, now, to start implementing systems that align with a sustainability model?

The "Problem" of Sustainability

If the nomads understand sustainability, then what is the big problem, and often pushback, that exists around understanding and implementing sustainability initiatives in the world and institutions today? To understand this better, I had some enlightening conversations with two pioneers, leaders, and practitioners in the corporate sustainability movement: Guy Bigwood and Andy Last.

Guy Bigwood, a pioneer and experienced practitioner in the corporate sustainability movement suggests, that the

> biggest change needed in organisations is a greater understanding of the importance of systems thinking. We live in a world of complex, dynamic, and interconnected systems that manage and provide for all aspects of our lives from the air we breathe, to the way we live in communities, to the way our financial systems work.

For nomads, this a normal mindset; their understanding of how systems work together is crystal clear. On that point, Guy translates this to the corporate environment.

> Today, in general, our literacy and understanding of these systems is low. We think in a very linear, siloed way and don't sufficiently understand and/or consider how our decisions affect other parts of the system, which has caused many of the problems we face. For business and society to become really sustainable, our leaders need to better understand and then make conscious decisions that consider how we interlink and interdepend on the financial, social, and environmental systems around us. Consequently, leaders need to expand their education and knowledge to think in a circular, systemic, and sustainable way.
>
> We have the same capacity to be interconnected, not just through technological methods of today, or communication, or relationships, but through our innate, deeper human capacity of social interactions with our environments. That is who we are. Just like the nomads and nature.

That is who we are. Just like the nomads and nature "

In many ways, this encourages a back-to-the-future sustainability thinking model that aligns with the nomadic mindset. Andy Last, CEO of MullenLowe, and author of *Business with a Mission*, consults with global, multinational organisations such as Unilever on sustainability. He explains,

> The shift we have seen in the world is a shift back in some ways. Businesses were founded based on a need by society, and you go back to the companies set up in the late nineteenth century in the USA and in the UK. They met a need in society, and leaders recognised the connection to society in terms of their employees. They needed to be looked after and their customers were in society; therefore, they needed to be cognisant of what was going on in society.

I think the shift that has happened over the last 30 years is that businesses became more beholden to the stock markets and the algorithms of stock markets and managing the short-term financial statement rather than the longer term of the growth of the business. With this, you see short-term leadership and the short-term holding of leaders.

Where is this short-termism leading to? What are the consequences?

Andy goes deeper into the social factor,

With the post-financial crash, growing understanding, the limits of the planet, the transparency driven by the internet, companies couldn't control or hide away a big part of their operations. And a younger generation coming into the workplace want more because they have grown up with the visibility of the internet. Plus, seeing social inequalities and the limits of the planet, all this is pushing business back, I believe, to having to understand its relationship with society and recognise that.

1. If the social factor is an issue here, especially with the millennial generation and younger, what are you doing to address this to attract the best and brightest talent?
2. What mindset(s) do you want your future employees to have?
3. Have you ever wondered who, in your corporation, will look at the system and sustainability?

Guy addresses what he has discovered on this question.

From experience, it is often the nomad who sees and starts to understand importance of systems thinking in an organisation. They move around the system first and see the effect on the people and planet. It seems that the nomads are frequently the instigators and key drivers of sustainability. The nomad then appreciates the roles of the builder and settler profiles to make their sustainability vision real.

They move around the system first and see the effect on the people and planet "

Who might those nomads be in your company? For a corporation to flourish as Guy suggests, it takes individuals with all three different mindset typologies to interconnect and migrate to a sustainable solution together. There is no magic formula to determine the quantity of individuals you need within a particular mindset dominance. It will depend on the vision and evolution of your institution at any particular time.

An organisation that appears to be upholding a "sustainability contract" is Unilever. Guy and Andy both say Paul Polman, CEO of Unilever, understands this. Unilever is one of the oldest multinational consumer goods corporations (established in 1929) and focuses on food, beverages, cleaning agents, and personal care products. Let's take a brief look at Paul's mindset and views on sustainability and the problems and possible solutions existing today.

Case Study: Unilever

Paul says,

> The world we want is an enormous responsibility. The very essence of capitalism is under threat as business is now seen as a personal wealth accumulator. We have to bring this world back to sanity and put the greater good ahead of self-interest. We need to fight very hard to create an environment out there that is more long-term focused and move away from short-termism. (Confino 2012)

If I reflect on nomads when considering long- versus short-termism, they have a long vision of their culture, the environment, when they may need to migrate (as the Mongolians), and what it takes for them as individuals and a community to live and sustain themselves. When it comes to their immediate goals of day-to day-living and grazing their animals, they believe if they overgraze a field or pasture, then it will take a long time to grow back again. Practicing sustainability, for them, is a natural occurrence.

On an organisational note, though, Guy shares that,

> Polman has driven the organisational transformation of Unilever towards sustainability while having to battle the financial world to do annual reporting instead of quarterly. He has challenged and made analysts and others realise that a longer-term strategy delivers better results.

How successful are you in trying to convince your shareholders, executive teams, and board of directors of long- versus short-termism? Are you bold enough to step into that discussion—perhaps disagreement?

Business Model Alignment

When speaking about sustainability, Paul suggests it comes down to the type of corporate business model you aspire to and how that aligns with your fiduciary duty. Does your business model align and integrate with your vision, values, and purpose? Is sustainability a driving centrepiece of that model? Do your strategies, financial instruments, and decisions align with your destination, or in this case, vision? Paul asserts,

> I don't think our fiduciary duty is to put shareholders first. I say the opposite. What we firmly believe is that if we focus our company on improving the lives of the world's citizens and come up with genuine sustainable solutions, we are more in synch with consumers and society, and ultimately, this will result in good shareholder returns. (Confino 2012)

1. When considering this quote, how important to you is sustainability within your business model?
2. Does improving the lives of world citizens interest you?
3. Can you see how this mindset could result in increased returns?

Paul's view relates to the qualities of the nomadic mindset. Guy says that Paul is one of those nomads who sees the linkage between the four pillars of sustainability (people, planet, profit, and culture). They are, in essence, the destination he has led Unilever towards with great success. It is one that drives interconnectivity—holistic and human focused. Now where does this nomadic vision and perspective come from? It starts with vision, values, qualities, and purpose.

As Paul says,

> The moment you discover in life that it's not about yourself, that it is about investing in others, I think you're entering a steadier state to be a great leader. Because above all, I think the main quality of a leader is to be a human being. There's no reason you are special because you happen to have this job or these responsibilities. (Cunningham 2015)

Get Out of the Way

In other words leaders, *get out of the way* and migrate to expansive thoughts from a human and economic perspective. The institution and its purpose are greater than you. What is needed is creating an environment of interconnectedness within companies at all levels and mindsets including external stakeholders, climate, and people. This comes down to alignment of why your corporation exists in the first place.

Sadly, though, if you look around you, you will see that myopism (narrow thinking) is rampant in much of the world's governments and organisations. While many corporations are implementing sustainability strategies and moving in the Unilever direction, conversations and research have suggested they are not going far enough fast enough. It takes bold, courageous leadership to make this happen.

Guy reiterates this belief, which reflects the Maasai ritual of becoming a warrior:

> We need more brave, bold, and courageous leaders who want to disrupt their industries and build more truly sustainable and regenerative businesses. Challenges to sustainability comes from many angles, and Wall Street is one of them: personal greed, wealth, and corruption play a large role that limits sustainable thinking and processes.

Are you solely filling the pockets of your shareholders or Wall Street? Or do you possess a more expansive picture of this thriving world?

Paul goes further when he refers to investors, "We must attract the right investors. If you buy into our approach to long-term value creation . . . then invest in us. If not, I respect you as a human being, but don't invest in us" (Bent 2010).

How bold and courageous are you as a leader to assert yourself to the lion? Are you willing to take on the responsibilities and put your life on the line?

It is worth repeating a couple quotes here that reflect responsibility: Benson Muntere, the Maasai warrior, said, "you cannot kill a lion alone; it takes everyone," and Paul Polman said, "the world we want is an enormous responsibility." What do you think?

you cannot kill a lion alone; it takes everyone 🙶

Sustainability needs Resilience as a Mindset Quality

Resilience Is Normal for Nomads

If you are to embody sustainability as part of your business model, it takes resilience to make it happen. Why? Because the sustainability pathway can be bumpy as you have come to realise. Where does this resilience comes from? Kwek Kok Kwong, CEO NTUC Learning Hub, Singapore, suggests it comes from nomads.

A nomad is somebody who is quite resilient and is constantly looking for ways to survive, looking for greener pastures, looking for the next place, not for only himself but the entire troupe, so there's a bit of that family thing, a bit of that wolf pack thing. We move together as a pack and we help, we look after each other, and it is our duty to make sure as a tribe, as a pack, we all survive.

For centuries, nomads have lived in disruption from droughts and wars to explorers exploiting them and using them as slaves, persecuting them as heathens and dirty uncivilized people, and systemic efforts to exterminate them as a society. Today, nomads still face a massive threat from climate change, government and developer land grabs, and the overdevelopment of tourism that simultaneously treats them as mascots or a circus show for tourists. Resilience is what has allowed them to sustain their life and culture and simply survive. It is part of that movement of the mind: the nomadic mindset.

❝ you have to be resilient and adapt fast

They are proud individuals and communities who want to preserve and sustain their culture while trading or doing business. They are continuing to adapt, though, as is their way, and they change when need be. This resilience and adaptation is how their mindset functions and responds to their environment. Just as Joel Soit, my Maasai friend, took the lion killing his cows in stride, you have to be resilient and adapt fast. This is normal for nomads. It is the nomadic mindset.

How normal is resilience for you?

A Resilient Organisation

A sustainable organisational culture is based on systems, people, culture, and nature being resilient: the bounce-back factor. It first takes the right mindset qualities to understand this and then implement what is needed within the culture. Some debate that people today have decreased resilience, and a primary reason may be because we are too comfortable and lack the hunger our nomadic ancestors needed to survive and thrive. Is this a first-world problem? Good question.

1. How resilient are you, your employees, or your organisation?
2. Who are the nomads in your company who have the resilience to courageously forge new innovations, strategies, and marketing ideas?
3. Think about what actionable steps you can develop to create a resilient corporate culture.

There is no, one, answer; however, it typically starts with executive leadership vision, mindset, actions, and interconnection with their systems. Some think that to build a resilient organisational culture, you need to have motivated, engaged employees interconnected with others, the vision, and the destination.

This plays directly into Andy Last's (CEO of MullenLowe) words, "The mindset is vital to be spoken about and observed as it is the single most [important determinant] of productivity and engagement of the workforce."

Engagement Interventions To Consider

There are multiple engagement interventions that companies are implementing that can assist in you sustaining a resilient corporation. These are some interventions to consider:

INTERVENTION 1

Provide a solid, comprehensive sustainability footprint that employees can engage with and undertake themselves through cooperation with other teams/tribes.

People are searching for a home or an institution they can belong to and grow with that supports their beliefs and purpose. They want to be part of a greater, expansive vision for humanity. This means an organisation needs a "walking the talk" set of sustainable principles.

Andy says,

This puts a number of different behaviours onto leaders, which is to be open to partnership with other players in society, whether it is government or not for profit, to demonstrate their companies' purpose, its right to exist in society, and the value it is bringing to society. This shows the openness of communication that business leaders need to show more vulnerability because they can't control everything that is going on. This doesn't actually play well with the players on Wall Street, but it plays well [with] the other stakeholders in society.

How can you enrich your sustainability footprint?

INTERVENTION 2

Create a culture that rewards independent, autonomous thinking.

Roland Genson, Director at the European Council has found,

> If you allow your people to lead with their own competences, you take a risk that you do not control anything, and things are moving all the time. And that, in my mind, is good. You are moving all the time, and nothing is stable. It is a way to get to targets and get motivated people; this is a way to reach a collective mindset where "change" is just considered as "normal."

In what ways does your organisation allow freedom to think?

INTERVENTION 3

Incorporate the qualities of a nomadic mindset, which lead to a resilient and motivated organisation.

Andy's business model concerns making a rational business case to understand sustainability and its value for a corporation's legacy and existence in today's world. He makes the case that "nomadic learning has been around a lot longer than capitalist learning, and this nomadic mindset is a way to motivate the workplace, which is a common [human resources] and leadership challenge in today's organisations."

nomadic learning has been around a lot longer than capitalist learning 🙿

What are the nomadic qualities you want embedded in your company?

INTERVENTION 4

Prioritize those with mindsets who are more entrepreneurial or intra-preneurial.

This is Andy's thought on this from what he has experienced in multinational organisations:

> We need new ways of prioritising mindsets and the mindsets for business. I definitely see big problems in the big, multinational companies who need to move towards being more entrepreneurial, and they all say they want to become more entrepreneurial with more people able to make decisions

while pushing down this decision making to the lowest level possible. This is very difficult in a hierarchical rule that follows structure, and therefore they speak about intra-preneurs. You don't hire an intra-preneur based on a skill set; it is absolutely a mindset.

What are the ways you can inspire entrepreneurial and intra-preneurial mindsets?

What you find in nomadic cultures is that they have to be entrepreneurial, independent, flexible, fast thinkers with a fluid system of interconnectedness within their environment and their internal and external communities. It was easy to observe this happening in the camel market in Morocco, with the Maasai at the food and goods market, with the Maasai women making beautiful, beaded jewellery then selling to it tourists, or the Mongolian nomad gathering his family together to shear the sheep to sell the wool for cashmere products.

INTERVENTION 5

Hire not just by skills but by the dominant mindset you need for that position.

Nothing disengages people more than fulfilling a role that doesn't fit with their why and mindset. Everyone can have the same skills yet not the same mindset to put those skills into action. The challenge of today is finding the right people with the right mindset for the right position so they remain motivated and engaged in their activities.

Identifying a person's mindset dominance (nomadic, builder, settler) by looking at their associated qualities and stories assists human resources managers and talent recruiters to better hire for a sustainable growing and thriving organisation. This will enrich the environment and culture dramatically by building more confidence.

In what ways can you identify the different mindset typologies?

Sustaining the Future of Organisations: Partnership Trend

The next destination and growing trend that will assist you in achieving sustainability is working in partnerships. Andy shares,

Mass communication is changing radically, and they are now having to stay aware and adaptable to all the channels of digital communication, which means partnering with all sorts of digital start-ups. There is a partnership motif playing out now. You see research and development is increasingly being driven by partnering with outside companies and not internally.

Is this a new trend, or is it a back-to-the-future quality of the nomadic mindset? Developing partnerships has been a defining quality of nomads for centuries. It is part of the nomadic spirit and mindset. If you think back to Indulge in the Tea Ceremony at the beginning of Part 2, you will remember partnerships are what has helped sustain cultures, networks, economies, safety, support, relationships, and communities. Perhaps, then, the ability to sustain sustainability is through resilient partnerships. What can you do to make building partnerships a new destination?

○

My partnership with Joel Soit, a Maasai warrior, to learn about their resilient, sustainable culture continues. One component of helping me complete part of this cultural exploration is seeing a hippo. I have seen four of the Big Five animals while in the Mara, yet I haven't seen the hippos.

As we walk through the Maasai Mara in search of hippos, Joel approaches two young nomads/herders of about five and eight and asks if they have seen any hippos. They nod their head and lead us to them. Ah, communication/partnership/resilience/sustainability/being better together.

What mindset does a sustainable organisation need for the future?

A balance of the nomadic, builder, and settler mindsets.

What mindset do organisations need more of in the future?

The answer is unanimously the nomadic mindset.

Guy says, "nomads are the drivers in sustainability." And sustainability is the interconnection of the nature of things.

○

Your final destination in returning home is to embrace one of the most important nomadic leadership qualities and principles: you can Never Settle . . . for Too Long. Just pause to reap the harvest of your achievements . . . then start the cycle again.

○ ○ ○

LEADERSHIP RETHINK

Essential nomadic leadership qualities to embody:

Ability to sustain	Growth	Adapt
Sustainability	Learn	Flexible
Interconnection	Inspire	Entrepreneur
Balance	Motivate	Intra-preneur
Values	Energize	Communication
Lead	Independent	Engage

FINAL QUESTIONS

1. What is a business model that will lead you to a more sustainable balance of mindset typologies?

2. What can you change so you integrate processes that will lead to a more resilient environment—starting with your people?

3. How important to you is having a business model that promotes sustainability?

Never Settle . . . for Too Long

"All you need is the plan—the road map—and the courage to press on to your destination"
– EARL NIGHTINGALE

OCTOBER 5, 2017, MONGOLIA

It is a chilly early fall afternoon out in the Mongolian steppes. My research team of Esso, Orgil, Baddy, Fredrik, and me are sitting on our beds in one of the three yurts our hosts, Namjildorj and Ravdan, own. The fire in the middle is blasting heat, and even still, we are dressed in all our warm clothes: fall is rapidly approaching. The weather is changing fast.

There is nothing outside but the owners' truck, a motorbike, an outhouse in the distance, a solar disc, two dogs, and a corral or pen for the goats and sheep. Off in the distance, you can see another yurt, which belongs to Raydan's father, who is 82 years old and still herding his camels on a horse.

In walks our hosts through a small door: Namjildori, smiling and wearing western clothes with high leather boots, and Raydan in his traditional blue coat—with long sleeves that double as hand warmers when he crosses his arms and puts his hands in the opposite sleeve—high leather boots, and a traditional hat. Esso talks with them and translates the answers to my questions. I ask them about their life, how many times they migrate each year, when do they know when to migrate, how long they settle before migrating, and more.

they sense things before us, yet we also sense the changes 🔊

Then, all of a sudden, Raydan gets up and rushes out in the middle of the conversation. The conversation continues with Namjildori. We find out they migrate two or three times per year, depending on the seasons and the weather. The animals indicate when to leave, she says, "they sense things before us, yet we also sense the changes." Then Raydan reappears. He needed to see to his livestock. He says each day they rotate their animals to different areas, so they don't overeat one area.

Then, again all of a sudden, they both leave the yurt with no real indication or reason why—they just leave. Later, I find out Raydan had to go and bring his animals back from the pasture and Namjildori needed to begin cooking dinner—for us!

Without watches, they sense the time of the day and understand intuitively the simple processes of the day. This made me more curious.

What I observed and learned was that even though they migrate physically to new areas, they also migrate in the movement of the mind. They were still, alert, and listening, yet they Never Settled . . . for Too Long, just long enough, while always being present wherever they were at that exact moment.

How important is it for you to Not Settle . . . for Too Long and still be present when considering your leadership or organisation?

You Have Arrived

You have now reached your final Destination for this journey: *The Nomadic Mindset™ . . . Never Settle . . . for Too Long.*

The qualities you have experienced through the nomadic stories are embedded in the nomads' cultures and mindset. No matter if you are in Mongolia or Kenya or Morocco, the qualities are the same. There is no secret; you are no different; these qualities are living vibrantly within you—you just may be on automatic pilot and have forgotten them.

> ❝ *you just may be on automatic pilot and have forgotten them*

This journey has invited you to migrate and expand to borderless perspectives and hopefully challenged you while encouraging you to explore the nomad in you through qualities such as migration, change, disruption, listening, stillness, alertness, Foie Gras, respect, trust, and solidarity. If they haven't already given you pause to reflect on your leadership, they certainly have the potential to create an impressive impact on you and enrich your overall leadership style.

Before we end this journey, though, there is one last important destination you want to discover that is both plaguing and driving Industry 4.0 today. That is Never Settle . . . for Too Long.

The Speed of Industry 4.0

Imagine the Formula 1 car race. You're likely picturing noisy cars driving at high speeds, never stopping. Once a Formula 1 car pulls into the pit, the team has to make sure it Never Settles . . . for Too Long—just long enough to change the tires, gas up, and fix anything—and even still, they are always trying to take milliseconds off the pit stop. They know if the car settles for too long, they will lose the race.

1. Is the speed of change what is challenging you as a leader?
2. If so, how does it make you feel?
3. What are you doing about it?

Today, this speed can drive individuals, teams, and corporations crazy . . . if you let it. This current reality is only going to get crazier as we move forwards. As you are all too aware, the acceleration of the speed of change, primarily prompted by Industry 4.0 with its technological innovations and digital transformation such as artificial intelligence, is increasing. Research has shown that, globally, a majority of leaders, organisations, and governments will be left behind and perhaps then become dinosaurs if they don't adapt to the multiple changing environments (Cegos Asia Pacific 2017).

And you may ask if you will become redundant with your current skills or mindset. The answer is possibly, and for some, most probably. But there is hope: Andy Last emphasizes "mindsets are not skills."

Everyone can have a variety of proficiency levels in similar skills; however, people do not necessarily have the same dominant mindset. Your mindset determines how you transform those skills and put them into action. As Andy Last explains, "Skills can be developed, and also, the skills that are relevant today won't necessarily be the same skills that are relevant in five, ten years' time. We need to have a mindset that is open to adapting and learning new skills." When Andy talks about "adapting," he is talking about people who lean towards a more nomadic mindset.

Never before have we had to create, innovate, and change so rapidly and so often

For this purpose, companies, governmental systems, and humans can Never Settle . . . for Too Long before something new appears, especially if you don't want to become irrelevant anytime soon. Never before have we had to create, innovate, and change so rapidly and so often. It can be daunting, as it is for some, but for others, it is an exuberating time.

One way of strategically tackling this is to develop a diverse culture of different mindset typologies: nomadic, builder, and settler, not only in your corporation but within you and your leadership style. This will give you the ability to sustain, understand the speed, and stay relevant while coping with the multiple technological, social, or cultural changes.

Adapting to Remain Relevant

Claire Smith, VP Marketing for the Vancouver Convention Centre, shares what they are doing:

> To push innovation, whether that's looking for new markets, new opportunities, or looking at new ways of monetizing different assets, we have been looking at re-imagining and repositioning some of the things we been doing for a long time, so I think we have a very nomadic appetite for the evolution of our settlement.
>
> It is an interesting combination of both, as I think we are very much a settlement, but we have that nomadic appetite. We look to global forces for

inspiration and innovation, particularly when I look from my role. I'm out there seeing what other people are doing, so I feel like the nomad going out into the world to see what we can bring back to our settlement. It's very much about having an open mind, a clear understanding that the world is changing, and that our business is evolving, and that if we don't continue to change, and if we became the settler, we could very much become irrelevant. That is always a threat, fear of our industry becoming irrelevant.

As Charles Darwin so famously said, "It's not the strongest of species that survives, nor the most intelligent, it's the one most adaptable to change." This is something nomads understand fully: being adaptable. What about you?

Leading and Managing in the Age of Disruption (2017), white paper by CEGOS, states the majority of leaders meant to be driving this transformation in corporations are slow to transform, and some are not interested at all. This can create more instability and disruption in markets, and the multi-generational divide may become more apparent. This could lead to even more human disruption, decreasing engagement and motivation, hence, productivity and human migration challenges.

> **❝ It's not the strongest of species that survives, nor the most intelligent, it's the one most adaptable to change**

These real challenges are already happening. For the sake of this book, it is about understanding and embracing a change of mindset that will help you stay relevant and transition and integrate into the new technological revolution. This change of mindset to a more nomadic one is about an expanded, flexible, adaptable state of being without borders, that is, living, breathing, and leading without mental and physical borders. As a human race, we are certainly great at building borders. This is where nomads can show us a better way forwards.

Nomads are so used to changes that when a new disruption occurs, they take it in stride, reflect upon it, and the elder intuitively gathers information and decides on a course of action. It is normal to change.

On the other hand, there are some leaders and companies moving rapidly and migrating to expansion of the mindset, and they are to be applauded as they lead the way. They are embracing the qualities of a nomadic mindset and encouraging this within their organisations. Some of these have been highlighted throughout this book: Unilever, Tata, Standard Charter, and Suntec Convention Centre. Other examples include Amazon, Apple, Alibaba Group, Mindshare World, and more.

1. Are you embracing change and the digital transformation?
2. How fast are you working towards this?
3. What are you doing to break down borders in your institution?

But First, Take Time to Harvest

Even while respecting that speed and having the right mindset are vital, a leader has to be intuitively interconnected to their internal and external environments so they strategically migrate at the appropriate time. Timing is paramount: not too soon and not too late to market. A fine line indeed. This takes the qualities of a nomad, just as Raydan, my Mongolian host, had. He intuitively knew when to move and tend to his livestock.

Robin Lokerman, Group President of MCI-Group, says,

> I think a successful business means you need to sow, innovate, and do things differently, but make sure that you take time to harvest that innovation before you innovate (sow) again. I believe value gets created while harvesting, but a successful harvest requires seeds of innovation to be planted first.

What he is saying is, remember: you must Never Settle . . . for Too Long, otherwise the risks are too high.

> Often you plant too many fields, you're sowing all the time, but because you're sowing all the time, you don't have time to harvest, so you need to make sure that you have some places where you're harvesting while you're sowing, while you're sowing in another spot, and if you can do that then you always eat. You need to focus a lot, get one product/innovation into a place that makes money, and then focus on the next one, make that into money, and then focus on the next one, and then make that into money.

you must Never Settle . . . for Too Long **"**

In Mongolia, they change their pastures daily, so they don't overharvest or overgraze the area, which is what Robin is saying.

These insights and strategies encourage you to deeply consider what some of the nomadic qualities are that can help drive migration and expansion of ideas and solutions.

A pastoral nomad, for example, is nimble, light, carries few possessions, and has relatively no attachments to temporal, physical, mental, or emotional things. When you ask a Mongolian nomad how long it takes to tear down and put up a yurt, you'll find it's twenty minutes. This is the same for the nomads in Southern Morocco. Light, nimble, and fast.

In this way, they are free and unbound by boundaries in the mind, body, spirit, or geography to move at the right moment. This is their intuitive ability to sustain a readiness and willingness to move at any given moment. They move *only* when it is absolutely necessary. Why? Because their survival is on the line, and the risks and threats can be a challenge for the clan or tribe and livestock, just like an institution.

> **❝ They move only when it is absolutely necessary.**

Robin underscores this point.

Nomads wanna be light, yes, and well, I think a builder (mindset) is actually trying to build up some assets, and I think that in that business you need to be light, but you also need to make sure you have assets that you continue to invest in the opportunities because they always take an investment.

Hence you need different mindsets in the right position in your corporation for different reasons.

1. How intuitive are you when it comes to seeing new pastures ahead?
2. What new strategies and qualities would help you migrate when the time is right?
3. What do you need to do in your organisation to make it nimbler and lighter?

This conversation around harvesting and Never Settling . . . for Too Long inspired Boris Nordenström, a multipreneur and angel capitalist from Stockholm to share this:

If you innovate all the processes all the time, you die because then you will never do anything. But you should innovate all processes sometimes, you have to innovate all processes. I think that's sort of a similar thing because you need to settle for a moment. You look at the nomads and most animals. There are very few animals who are always travelling; some are I'm sure. But I'm sure there are some nomads that actually always travel, but most nomads have a period of travel and periods of settling. And when you reach a fantastic place, you stay for a while.

A fine example of Never Settling . . . for Too Long is the current darling of the tech industry (in some minds): Apple. Theirs is the story of a fluctuating, trillion-dollar company that rose, fell, and rose again under the leadership of Steve Jobs, a true nomad. This is an interesting story on many levels, but we shall look at it from a mindset perspective. You will see through the case study below how the current conversation revolves around the potential demise of Apple in the future if they don't change their mindset—very curious indeed.

Case Study: Apple

Boris Nordenström challenges us to look at Apple and its survival in the long term.

> The CEO of Apple right now is Tim Cook, who is an amazing incremental-ist, probably the best incrementalist (builder) on the planet. He is nowhere an innovator (nomad) in my view. Now of course, he has the playbook as he's been trained by Steve Jobs (nomad) to look for innovation, to understand innovation and all this stuff, but he just doesn't have a nomadic mindset; for him, it is about doing things a little better all the time.

I ask, *then why is Apple still so successful*? Boris doesn't think it is, actually, because of a lack of innovation. Boris ponders this as he continues:

> Yes, Steve Jobs did some amazing innovations with the iPhone and other products, but he would have been enormously good at incrementalism . . . if you take the iPhone 1 and put it next to the iPhone 7, there's no real difference, just a little bigger, and of course the inside is dramatically different, but it looks exactly the same! So, it is pure incrementalism. There's no innovation going on there, yet on the lower level, there's tons and tons of innovation.

So, Boris thinks one of the reasons Apple, unfortunately, is not going be part of the future is because he hasn't seen any innovation coming out of Apple for a long time now. He doesn't even remember the last time they innovated anything on a higher level. A curious insight, don't you think? I ask another Swedish executive, Tahero Nori, the COO and founder of TechBuddy, his opinion.

> Apple knows what to deal with, but that was thanks to Steve Jobs because if you look at what Tim is doing, he doesn't have innovative products at all, but he's a very good operational guy. If you [had] Steve Jobs, Apple would be the most valuable company in the world (and it is up there with Amazon in numbers). Steve Jobs had innovated so much that they would be living as kings [for] the next ten years.

The problem is that they are bringing so many fragments of people from the different verticals from the industry that the vision is not clear anymore. Look at the products that they [made] . . . this touchpad, it's ugly; Steve jobs would never allow that. In my opinion, they have lost the vision, definitely the vision.

Both opinions are thought-provoking, whether or not you agree with them. I challenge you to take an expansive step back with the Eyes of a Hawk and consider what they are saying. These are opinions you must contemplate if you are to survive, sustain, and thrive.

1. What mindset do you think Apple is in now: nomadic, builder, or settler?
2. What potential comparisons can you draw from these observations to the Nokia success and failure story?
3. What new visionary pastures does Apple need to innovate and develop?

Now turn that around and look at your corporation and leadership and ask yourself this:

1. When was the last time you deeply looked at your vision and purpose as a leader or an institution?
2. What mindset are you and your company currently in, and for how long have you been there?
3. What do you need to do stay relevant, innovative, and sustainable?

If it has been over six months since you asked these questions, you might want to reflect upon them now. Never Settle . . . for Too Long.

Building Bubbles

If you are to avoid the challenge of overstaying your welcome in a pasture due to a lack of innovation, creativity, or mindset, who in your organisation needs to make those crucial decisions? Robin Lokerman says,

For companies to keep innovating and establishing a culture of innovation, it all comes down to the leadership—the right leader—so the CEO is critical. Then, of course, the board supporting that with a single management team helping [them] execute. If the CEO doesn't set the right vision for the company and the drive for innovation, plus do things differently by seeking new opportunities, then it's very hard to sustain the business in the long run.

Hence, you are potentially heading towards dinosaurville. Never Settle . . . for Too Long, is a mindset quality of an individual, corporation, or government with a nomadic mindset. This quality is one of the most important qualities you need for the mindset of the future. It has no boundaries and keeps you on the edge of success and migrating, innovating, and expanding when necessary.

Robin shares another example of a leadership strategy and mindset used in Dubai leadership. As you may know, their origins are not many years from their nomadic roots, living in the desert as a trading culture.

> I read a book called *Leadership Dubai Style*, by Tommy Weir, and one of the habits Tommy has identified is called 'playing with bubbles.' The Dubai leadership create a bubble, and they know the bubble will burst, but when the bubble bursts, they always have a new bubble, so they continuously are creating a vision and opportunity . . . When the stock market burst in 2008, they had a bigger bubble that allowed the world to work towards these new things. They are continuously in a new bubble that the leadership is building on. I think that is where you continuously need to have a new vision to be continuously new. Something you strive for. I think that's all forwards looking, and I think a lot of European cultures and businesses are actually backwards looking, and that's even worse than the status quo, that's retro-focused. I think that's completely the wrong mindset.

Never Settle . . . for Too Long 🙶

If you look at the Dubai leadership style from an expanded view, it is an example of a nomadic mindset, with a team of builder mindsets who drive the innovation and vision while those with a dominant settler mindset are the glue that keep it on track and together. It is this combination of mindsets that makes the institution thrive. Then it takes the right communication to drive success. Never Settle . . . for Too Long.

Change the Conversation

If you Never Settle . . . for Too Long, then you can keep conversations moving, flowing, changing, and adapting.

Claire Smith, VP Marketing with the Vancouver Convention Centre agrees:

> I really want to change the conversation with all of our clients about really what are the outcomes they are hoping to achieve. If we start with the outcome, and we work back from there, we can have a powerful conversation

rather than a conversation around wants and needs. Let's focus on what success would look like and what kind of outcomes our audience is hoping to achieve.

Today, due to the speed of Industry 4.0, do you get the feeling you are sometimes not gently prompted, but rather provoked and forced to change the conversation and pasture if you are to sustain your relevance, survive, and thrive?

Then I invite you to change the conversation around what you want your organisational culture to be. You can get back on plot, if you had indeed slipped off, by musing and integrating the qualities of the nomadic mindset while maintaining a balance of all the mindsets: nomadic, builder, and settler.

○

Raydan, the kind Mongolian nomad who shared one of his yurts with my team, told me it would not be long, maybe a few days or a couple of weeks, before they would migrate to their winter pastures. They would then rest out the winter surrounded by mountains, so their livestock would not freeze from the icy cold winds. Then once winter melts away, in early spring, they will be off again to different pastures. Never Settling . . . for Too Long—just long enough.

○ ○ ○

LEADERSHIP RETHINK

Essential nomadic leadership qualities to embody:

Observation	Understanding	Vision
Intention	Adaptation	Communication
Conversation	Innovation	Sharing
Leadership	Borderless	Harvesting
Outcome	Clarity	Never Settle . . .
Mindsets	Future	for Too Long

FINAL QUESTIONS

1. What if you Never Settle . . . for Too Long? What can that do for you?

2. What if you Never Settle . . . for Too Long? How can that change your conversations?

3. What if you Never Settle . . . for Too Long? What can that do for the future of your organisation?

RETHINK

PART 5

Distillation

◉

*"I've learned that people will forget what you said,
people will forget what you did, but people
will never forget how you made them feel"*

– MAYA ANGELOU

Photo by Orgil Batsaikhan

It is time to say so long for now, and before we part

company on this journey, here is a little recap—

a Distillation—of where we have migrated from and to.

BEFORE YOU GO

Now you have arrived at the Distillation point of *The Nomadic Mindset*™: *Never Settle . . . for Too Long*. How do you feel now? Do you sense more expansion?

It's time to pause this nomadic journey to Rethink and dig deeper into your newly acquired gems of wisdom, then take action on how you want to adapt this ancient wisdom and these story-filled metaphors to your leadership path.

Along the way, you have been introduced to the three mindset typologies—nomadic, builder, settler—and the qualities associated with them. They all exist within each one of us, in every organisation and every systemic evolution. You have probably found each one of them within you, with less or more of one than the others.

Many of the associated rich stories and qualities associated with *The Nomadic Mindset*™ you will have experienced before from a different perspective. But now from now on, I offer you a different lens to see them through.

If you Never Settle . . . for Too Long,
make sure you settle long enough to reap the harvest
of these five beautiful quotes and proverbs, gifts
from Mongolia, Kenya, and Morocco.
They will empower as you journey to The Nomadic Mindset.

○

Nomad = The movement of the mind
Mindset is your capital.
You can't put the whole camel in the pot at one time, only one piece at time.
We are migrating . . . where we were is not where we are.
Think vastly; act narrowly.

○

Now ask yourself,

1. What did I discover that could get me back on plot?
2. How can this fresh new mindset leadership path be of benefit to me and my organisation?
3. What are my next steps in applying this wisdom?

○

It's now up to you as a leader to thrive and flourish with the ancient nomadic wisdom that has transcended time.

The nomad exists within you and outside you as all things are interconnected. From time to time, meander back through these pages and discover them again in a different way.

RELIVE

Migrate to Expansion

there is no beginning to your journey
there is no ending to your journey

you are migrating
to expansion

there is no beginning to your leadership
there is no ending to your leadership

you are migrating
to expansion

there is no beginning to who you are
there is no ending to who you are

you are migrating
to expansion

migrate to expansion
to live in the nomadic mindset, to never settle . . . for too long.
in your mind, always move, always expand, to discover better routes and
greener pastures;
this is where great leaders thrive.

are you ready to migrate to expansion?

take a deep breath, look to your horizons,
and step into the nomadic mindset . . .

**Embrace the spirit of the nomadic leader in you today as today is
your future.**

Go nomading!

NOMADIC CONTRIBUTORS

With deep and heartfelt gratitude for your wisdom and enlightening me on nomadic ways and leadership, I am truly thankful for your participation in this ever-growing and changing project. This is just the beginning as there is no end.

Don't skip this rolling-credits thank-you list of contributors!

Mongolia

Esso Khulan Baljinnyam
Tuya Shagdar
Nergui Sandagjav
Myagmarsuren Gantumur
Batgerel Bat

Binderiya Davaanyam Bat
Orgil Batsaikhan
Batsaikhan Baljinnyam
Namjildorj Oyun
Ravdan Sanduijav

Kenya

Pierina Redler
Joel Soit
Saruni Nick Kaleku
Benson Kipolonka Muntere
Mary Soit

Oloodo Soit
Lilian Naisola Malo
James Koileken
Simon Soitanae

Morocco

Pedro Paquemar
Sarah Lina Hata
Hicham Zemmer
Romain Simenel
Aissa Derhem
Brahim Tahero

Habib El Ballayni
Ali Bellini
Mohamed Billa
Salem Manchette
Bamal Boujemaa
Mohamed Blaoui

EXECUTIVE WISDOM CONTRIBUTORS

As executives, you have been incredibly generous with me in our conversations. I am deeply grateful to you for your time, energy, and interest in *The Nomadic Mindset*™: *Never Settle . . . for Too Long* and desire to make a difference in the world.

You may not all be quoted in the in the book, and I apologize for that. In fact, there is enough information for another book. Our conversations have helped shape and transform my mindset, content, and overall knowledge about leadership. You all have played a constructive role in defining the qualities associated with the mindset typologies, which will become an assessment tool in early 2019. Again, thank you for your generosity—I am humbled.

Robin Alfred
Muhammed Adnan Azam
Esso Khulan Baljinnyam
Guy Bigwood
Jeremy Blain
Genoveva Ruiz Calavera
Aissa Derhem
Xavier Desaulles
Tanvi Gautam
Roland Genson
Dr. Bill Hanlon
Karoli Hindriks
Richard Huggins
Cristian Jonsson
Kwek Kok Kwong
Andy Last
Maurice Levine
Linda Georgina Locke
Robin Lokerman
Tim Love
Arun Madhok
Krista Monson
Boris Nordenström

Tahero Nori
Dr. Sheila Patel
Steen Puggaard
Grant Axe Rawlinson
Dr. Barney Reeves
John Russell
Nergui Sandagjav
Elif Schmidt
Dr. Andrew Schuster
Hema Sedehey
Vikram Sharma
Claire Smith
Ashutosh Srivastava
Rohit Talwar
Agnes Tarnai
Michael Teoh
Bojan Tercon
Samuel Tan
Wendy Tan
Martina Valkovicova
Chris Van der Schoor
Mads Winblad
Said Zaki

AFTERWORD

To be a nomad is to be in search of something better. That is, literally, what the word means:

> "Nomad: late 16th century, from French *nomade*, via Latin from Greek *nomas*, nomad- 'roaming in search of pasture,' from the base of *nemein* 'to pasture.'"

The first time I met Kevin, I felt he had the nomadic mindset. A soul in search of something. In search—not of something missing—of a way to improve. And not to improve because something was not right, but to improve to make something even better.

Kevin's whole being is about calmly and slowly becoming better. To see him embrace the idea of understanding, describing, and spreading the idea and message of the nomadic mindset has been a joy.

I hope this book has inspired you, too, to always be on the move in your mind.

To always be looking at ways to become better.

To never stop looking for better pastures.

Fredrik Härén
The Idea Book and ProfessionalSpeaking.com

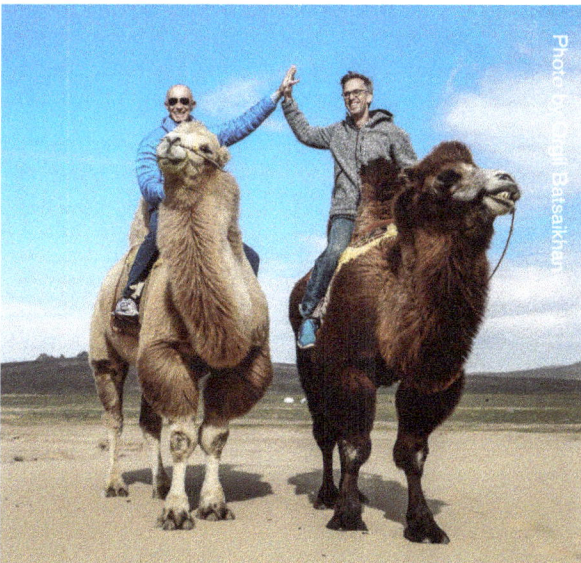

Photo by Gigi Batsaikhan

THE BEGINNING IS AT THE END

March 31, 2017, Singapore

My first meeting with my mentor, Fredrik Härén, was at his beautiful, large, colonial "Black and White House," which is typical in parts of old Singapore.

Having spent a good amount of time in Singapore over the past seven years, I've become more familiar with Fredrik, and admire his work as a Global Conferences Keynote Speaker. He is a master at developing your inner theme and connecting your why with what is driving you. This meeting is my moment of truth to find my inner theme.

I tell him I had recently accepted, after many years, my new brand: Global Nomad. His curiosity is piquéd, and I just go along for the ride, not completely registering where this conversation is heading.

I find myself telling him about the nomadic mindset, and Fredrik's reaction is this: "Wow, Kevin, what a great subject! I have never heard of this subject before. You need to write a book."

The more we talk, the more animated Fredrik becomes. He tells me "You need to go and spend time researching and spending time with nomads and have one hundred conversations with executives."

Oh my god, what have I gotten myself into now, I think. Fredrik senses my trepidation and says, "if you don't do this within the next year, I am going to do it—it's a great theme."

The journey to *The Nomadic Mindset*™ was born that day, with Fredrik kicking my butt into gear (thank you for that, Fredrik). What you're holding in your hand now is only part of the journey—there is always more to discover. Getting here has been one of the toughest projects of my life, while at the same time, it has been life changing. It has given me a new lease on life and purposeful direction. I sincerely hope it has come at a moment in your life when you need to migrate to expansion as a leader or organisation, then you can act with tenacity, strategy, and narrow focus.

The learning here is rich, and if you find much of it familiar, it is because you are tuning into your nomadic mindset: you are interconnected to the nature of things.

REFERENCES

Bent, David. 2010. "Choice quotes from the Unilever Sustainable Living Plan launch." *David Bent* (blog), November 16, 2010. https://davidbent.wordpress.com/2010/11/16/choice-quotes-from-the-unilever-sustainable-living-plan-launch/.

CEGOS. *Leading and Managing in the Age of Disruption: Responses and findings from the CEGOS survey of professionals across the Asia Pacific region*. Singapore: 2017. https://www.thenomadicmindset.com/wp-content/uploads/2019/01/Leading_and_Managing_in_the_Age_of_Disruption_Cegos.pdf

Collins Dictionary, s.v. "congested," accessed May 13, 2018, https://www.collinsdictionary.com/dictionary/english/congested

Confino, Jo. 2012. "Unilever's Paul Polman: challenging the corporate status quo." *The Guardian*, April 24, 2012. https://www.theguardian.com/sustainable-business/paul-polman-unilever-sustainable-living-plan.

Confino, Jo. 2012. "Rio+20: Unilever CEO on the need to battle on to save the world." *The Guardian*, June 21, 2012. https://www.theguardian.com/sustainable-business/rio-20-unilever-battle-save-world.

Cunningham, Lillian. 2015. "Unilever chief Paul Polman wants to orient company for the long term." *The Sydney Morning Herald*, May 25, 2015. https://www.smh.com.au/business/unilever-chief-paul-polman-wants-to-orient-company-for-the-long-term-20150525-gh8x7e.html.

Finke, Jens. n.d. "Maasai – Age-sets." Accessed December 31, 2018. http://www.bluegecko.org/kenya/tribes/maasai/agesets.htm

Merriam-Webster Dictionary, s.v. "culture," accessed May 25, 2018, https://www.merriam-webster.com/dictionary/culture

Nomad. 2018. *Wikipedia, The Free Encyclopedia*. Accessed December 31, 2018, https://en.wikipedia.org/wiki/Nomad

Oxford English Dictionary, s.v. "migration," accessed March 5, 2018, https://en.oxforddictionaries.com/definition/migration

Scialpi, Davide. 2018. "Paul Polman's quotes about Success and Leadership—CEO of Unilever." May 13, 2018. https://medium.com/@davidescialpi/paul-polmans-quotes-about-success-and-leadership-ceo-of-unilever-52aff401a105

Tata Group. 2019. *Wikipedia, The Free Encyclopedia*. Accessed December 31, 2018, https://en.wikipedia.org/w/index.php?title=Tata_Group&oldid=876500567

Usborne, David. January 20, 2012. "The moment it all went wrong for Kodak." *The Independent*. https://www.independent.co.uk/news/business/analysis-and-features/the-moment-it-all-went-wrong-for-kodak-6292212.html

Unity. 2018. *Wikipedia, The Free Encyclopedia*. Accessed December 31, 2018, https://en.wikipedia.org/wiki/Unity

GO NOMADING!

If you have found value in this book, please share it and the movement with others. You can connect with us at

connect@thenomadicmindset.com

If you are interested in how to better achieve new "pastures" and integrate your discoveries, feel free to contact us about inspirational keynotes, executive coaching, workshops, retreats, and more.

I invite you also to connect with me on

Linkedin: Kevin Cottam https://bit.ly/2ElPwbl
Youtube: The Nomadic Mindset

As I am continuing my executive interviews, I would be grateful to hear from you. If you would like to be interviewed for further blogs about The Nomadic Mindset contact

connect@thenomadicmindset.com

PRODUCTS TO WATCH FOR

The Nomadic Mindset™: Never Settle . . . for Too Long

the paperback and e-book

The Nomadic Mindset Dominance Assessment

(Determining your dominant mindset: nomadic, builder, or settler)

The Nomadic Mindset Workshops

Images of The Nomadic Mindset

(a partner coffee table book to the leadership book)

The Nomadic Mindset Online Course

The Nomadic Mindset Leadership Retreat

and more!

Lastly, stay in touch by joining us for more updates and information at

www.thenomadicmindset.com

ABOUT THE AUTHOR

Kevin Cottam, Canadian and Global Nomad. Based in Canada with outposts in Singapore, Brussels, and Lisbon, his mission is to inspire and encourage others to remove borders and expand their mindset: two primary qualities of a nomadic mindset.

From his early beginnings as a champion figure skater, a former elite figure skating choreographer for world and Olympic champions, and a director of large-scale productions such as the 1988 Olympic Closing Ceremonies, Kevin has naturally sought to expand his students' and audiences' creativity and flexibility by presenting story-rich visual experiences. Today, he continues his mission by inspiring leaders in multinational enterprises (e.g., Thales, Givaudan, Club Med, L'Oreal, Nestle) and public sector (European Union) environments as a global inspirational keynote speaker, executive coach, and trainer, so he can further touch more cultures, people, and organisations.

He is also author of *Aha, Mother's Pearls*, a self-help book filled with over twenty personal *Aha* moments of realisation.

www.thenomadicmindset.com